WITHDRAWN

THE EDUCATIONAL IDEAS OF
CHARLES FOURIER
(1772 – 1837)

THE EDUCATIONAL IDEAS OF CHARLES FOURIER
(1772–1837)

DAVID ZELDIN

AUGUSTUS M. KELLEY · PUBLISHERS
New York 1969

First published in 1969 by
FRANK CASS & COMPANY LIMITED
67 Great Russell Street, London W.C.1

Copyright © 1969 David Zeldin

Published in the United States by
Augustus M. Kelley, Publishers
New York, New York 10010

Library of Congress Catalog Card No. 67-31331

SBN 678 05019 8

Printed in Great Britain

Contents

Acknowledgments	vii
List of Abbreviations	viii
Introduction	1
1. Fourier's Life	5
2. The Psychological Basis of Fourier's Educational Thought	19
3. The Aims of Education	31
4. Parents and Teachers: the Organization of Teaching	51
5. Education and Care during Infancy: a Period for the Discovery of Vocation	67
6. Five to Ten Years	83
7. The Teenage Period: a Time for Social Service	97
8. Growing Up: the Problem of Sex and Education	119
9. Intellectual Education: an Approach to Academic Studies	127
10. Conclusion	143
Bibliography	155
Index	165

Acknowledgments

I SHOULD like to express my gratitude and indebtedness to my teachers and friends without whose generous help this book could not have been written: Professor V. Mallinson, for his very helpful comments and criticisms of an earlier draft; Dr. P. S. Bagwell, Dr. P. M. McGurk, and Professor B. Wilson, for their invaluable encouragement and advice.

I am also grateful to the Editors of *Paedagogiga Historica* for allowing me to use in Chapter 7 material from my article in volume v (1965) no. 2 of that journal.

D.Z.

List of Abbreviations

Abbreviations in the footnotes refer to the Complete Works of C. Fourier

Théorie des Quatres Mouvements (1841 ed.)	Q. M.
Théorie de l'Unité Universelle (in 4 volumes, 1843 ed.)	
Vol. One	
Libre arbitre	U. U., i, L.
Le Sommaire	U. U., i, S.
Avant-Propos	U. U., i, A.
Vol. Two	U. U., ii
Vol. Three	U. U., iii
Vol. Four	U. U., iv
Le Nouveau Monde industriel et sociétaire (1848 ed.)	N. M.
Publication des Manuscrits de C. Fourier. In 4 volumes: 1851; 1852; 1853–6; 1857–8	Manus. (followed by the year of publication).

Introduction

THE ideas of Charles Fourier have long fascinated economists, sociologists and political scientists.[1] Children play a most important part in his Utopian schemes. He devotes a whole volume to a thorough discussion of education, and elsewhere too gives it much prominence. Yet the educational theory of Fourier is a neglected and indeed almost unknown subject. He is primarily remembered as a social reformer, and his ideas have been considered significant largely for their influence on communist theory and in the co-operative movement.

The historians of education remain almost silent about him. Gabriel Compayré[2] mentions him only briefly and contemptuously. "Fourier", he writes, "had educational pretensions. There is nothing more curious than his treatise on 'Natural Education'. In it there is only here and there a flash of good sense mingled with a multitude of grotesque fancies.[3] There is little of practical value to be gathered from the writings of the celebrated utopists . . . It is the chimerical which characterizes their systems."[4] He concludes, "The education of the Fourierists is neither a discipline nor a rule of life; it is simply a system of complaisant adherence, and even ardent provocation, to the instincts which the child inherits from nature. It is no longer a question either of directing or of training, it is simply necessary to emancipate and excite."[5] Even when allowance is made for Compayré's conservatism and his unsympathetic approach, his judgment on Fourier's educational thought does not reflect any careful study.[6]

Discussing Froebel and his predecessors, Octave Gréard (Vice Recteur de l'Académie de Paris), in his monumental *Education et Instruction*, says that one must mention Fourier "qui dans son *Education harmonienne* (section troisième, conférence notice) developpe les mêmes principes sous une forme parfois étrange mais avec un sens profond des besoins de l'éducation de la *basse enfance*".[7] He however gives no further details or criticisms.

Buisson's *Nouveau dictionnaire de pédagogie*[8] admits that Fourier had a lot to say on education; it has a sympathetic article about him, but one too brief to allow it to come to grips with his educational ideas.

The Soviet Encyclopaedia[9] has a special section of its article on Fourier devoted to "Fourier's pedagogic ideas". It says that, although he was not aware of the Marxist class struggle, nevertheless, "Fourier . . . has many valuable educational ideas".[10]

Utopian thought has never been irrelevant in the conduct and planning of the affairs of men. "Past utopias have certainly had a notable effect on the minds of men even though none have ever been completely realized. The direct effect—of Plato on Dionysius or even of Marx on Lenin—has probably been less important than the indirect effects of robust dreams on the hopes and aspirations of man."[11] "Without the Utopians of other times", says Anatole France, "men would still live in caves, miserable and naked. It was Utopians who traced the lines of the first city . . . Out of generous dreams come beneficial realities. Utopia is the better principle of progress, and the essay into a better future."[12]

So too in educational practice, ideas are developed and advocated well before society can or will accept them. The neglect of Fourier as an educational theorist is not surprising. His educational ideas and innovations were well in advance of his time and were based on a view of society then (and perhaps even now) not generally acceptable. The education Fourier advocated and the educational problems he discussed seemed hardly relevant or even sensible to many theorists and educational practitioners. True, many of his ideas remain irrelevant and incomprehensible,[13] but, on the other hand, one is frequently struck by the topical nature of his ideas, the relevance to our age of the problems he discusses, and the surprising parallels with new experiments in educational methods.

The scope of Fourier's writing is immense[14] and this book sets out only those aspects of his theories which affect or explain his educational ideas. His educational ideas are interesting and important enough to be studied for their own sake.

1. See for example C. Gide and C. Rist, *History of Economic Doctrines* (1961); G. D. H. Cole, *History of Socialism* Vol. 1 (1953); F. Jollivet-Castelot, *Le Fourierisme et Sociologie* (1908); A. Pinloche, *Fourier et le socialisme* (1933); Martin Buber, *Paths in Utopia* (1949).
2. *The History of Pedgagogy* (1903). Translated by W. H. Payne.
3. Ibid., 528.
4. Ibid., 527.
5. Ibid., 529.
6. Cp. G. Cogniot, *La Question Scolaire* (1948). Compayré shows, Cogniot claims, "des préjugés ignorants et des mépris simplistes que la science officielle de l'éducation a obstinément opposés aus vues novatrices des saint-simoniens, des fourieristes, des icariens, en général des écoles socialites et communistes de la première moitié du XIXe siècle", 16.
7. *Education et Instruction*, vol. I, *Enseignement primaire* (1889, 2nd ed.), 9n.
8. Buisson (1911). Fourier "donne dans son système une large place à l'éducation", 646–648.
9. *Great Soviet Encyclopaedia* (1956), Vol. 45, 666–8. For the passage of his ideas into Russia, see Martin Malis, *Alexandre Herzen and the Birth of Russian Socialism, 1812–1855* (1961), 321–8. For a more detailed Soviet assessment see Introduction in *Isbrannyye sochineniya* [*Collected Works of Fourier*], Moscow, 1951, 4 vols.
10. Cp. B. Holmes, *Some Considerations of Method in Comparative Education*, Ph.D. Thesis, London 1962. "Soviet educators acknowledge Thomas More, John Bellers, Comenius, Rousseau and Pestalozzi, as well as the 'great Utopian socialists' C. Fourier and R. Owen, as having anticipated in their writings some of the ideas advocated by Marx and Lenin. In general the aim is to abolish the deforming divorce between mental and manual labour, or in educational terms, to bridge the gap between general education and vocational training." 387.
11. Philip Toynbee in *The Observer*, 1 April 1962; he goes on ". . . and it might reasonably be held that any political, or indeed religious, thinker ought to have some clear notion of the kind of human society which he believes to be desirable. Mr. Eliot was responding to this demand when he wrote his own kind of wry utopia in 'The Idea of a Christian Society'."
12. Quoted by Lewis Mumford, *The Story of Utopias* (1923), 22.
13. William Boyd has written "There are many curious ideas . . . in the education dreams of the time . . . it would be a mistake to lose sight of the wisdom that mingled with the folly". *The History of Western Education* (1950, 5th ed.), 364. See also H. C. Barnard, *The French Tradition in Education* (1922), where he writes "The history of education in France affords an extensive and profitable field for research. Much work has already been accomplished . . . but there are many aspects of the subject which have not yet been presented to readers in this country or even, in any detail,

in France itself", pp. v-vi. This is certainly true in the case of the educational ideas of Charles Fourier forty years after the above was written.

14. See for example, Martin Buber, *Paths in Utopia* (1949); D. O. Evans, *Social Romanticism in France* (1951), particularly pp. 48–51; and M. Friedberg, *L'influence de Charles Fourier sur le Mouvement Social Contemporain en France* (1926).

CHAPTER ONE

Fourier's Life

FRANÇOIS MARIE CHARLES FOURIER,[1] the son of Charles and of Marie Muguet, was born at Besançon, on 7 April 1772; he died in Paris on 7 October 1837.[2] The Fouriers were neither poor nor obscure as is usually thought. His father was a merchant of sufficient standing to have been elected "premier juge consulaire" for the year 1776, a post later equivalent to that of the President of the Tribunal of Commerce.[3] The Muguets, his mother's family, were rich, noble and with much influence in Besançon. One of the family was a member of the Constituent Assembly.[4]

Charles was the youngest of four children; the others, all girls, were to marry men of some consequence: Rubat, who was to become a sub-prefect;[5] Clarc, later a member of the Revolutionary Committee of Besançon;[6] and Brillat,[7] a relation of the celebrated gastronome Brillat-Savarin.[8]

His parents were comparatively rich, yet a series of misfortunes was soon to cripple him financially and he was to remain poor for the rest of his life. His father's early death and the subsequent mismanagement of his mother's affairs by a friend of the family at the time of the revolution account for the family's decline in fortune.[9] His own inheritance, which he invested in colonial produce, he partly lost during the siege of Lyons, and the remainder, some years later, during a storm at sea, when the cargo perished.[10]

He was never to allow his poverty to demoralize him. He remained calm and unruffled amid his misfortunes. Painstaking and determined, he was too regular in his habits to decay in distress. He always kept his coat carefully brushed, and wore a white necktie. If we may judge by anecdotes related of him he was genuinely kind and loved to help without seeking any reward or renown.[11]

Little is known of the early life of Charles Fourier. Taciturn and reserved, he was not inclined to reminisce, and when he did tell of his early life it was usually to illustrate some point of his theory.[12] He was educated at the College of Besançon, and he received a classical education,[13] an education "formelle et banale qu'on donnait alors".[14] At school he seems to have done very well. The annual register of Besançon for 1786, the only one of that time which mentions college prizes, shows Charles to have won the two highest prizes for composition and Latin poetry in the 3rd class.[15] He was an intelligent and persevering child, but already somewhat given to self-sufficiency and day-dreaming.[16] Charles had early set his heart on a career as an engineer. Encouraged by his relationship with the Blessed Jean-Pierre Fourier,[17] he had hoped to secure entrance to the then exclusive school of military engineering at Mézières.[18] His mother had however refused, on account of the expense, to buy the necessary letters of nobility. Instead he was destined to lead the most prosaic life imaginable—that of a commercial traveller. He left school before he was eighteen, and was almost immediately apprenticed to a merchant in Rouen to learn the cloth business.[19] But he was never to remain long in any one position; his passionate love of travel and his intense desire for new knowledge and more time for study made him frequently change master and abode. He was thus to hold a variety of positions as commercial traveller, broker and clerk in the cloth houses, mostly in Lyons, but also in Rouen, Marseilles, Bordeaux,[20] and in the last ten years of his life in Paris.[21] He also travelled widely in Germany, the Netherlands and later in Switzerland, as well as in France.[22] Intelligent, observant, full of curiosity, with a retentive memory and not afraid of asking questions nor of spending time in solitary study, Fourier soon accumulated a considerable knowledge and experience.

Living amidst the tumultuous times of the French Revolution, Fourier took a keen interest in his surroundings and in the events of the day, often visiting the reading rooms in his spare moments for the latest news and theories. However he devoted himself mainly to contemplation and study: he remained aloof from political intrigue.[23] He never thought to have his system adopted other than by persuasion: never by force, governmental authority, or coercive power of any sort.

He suffered much during the Reign of Terror: he was arrested several times and narrowly escaped the guillotine.[24] During the Insurrection of Lyons he had lost most of his worldly goods. Yet his misfortunes seem in no way to have affected his belief in the eventual perfectibility of man. Although he witnessed so much wretchedness, cruelty and extreme suffering, Fourier, an unmitigated optimist, firmly held to his belief that pain, illness, and misery were totally unnecessary; and that their complete destruction was a practical possibility.

In 1793[25] he was drafted into the 8th Regiment of Cavalry, commanded by a cousin of his by marriage, Colonel Brincour,[26] where he remained until invalided out two years later. His army life was never arduous. For the rest of his days, though no man had a more pacific nature, Fourier loved to follow regiments of soldiers through the streets, to keep time to the sound of military music. He spent long hours watching soldiers drill, not from any warlike taste, but because he loved ceremony, parades, uniforms, plumes and decorations. Here we find the germ of his ideas for the organization of the Petites Hordes.

Fourier's activities and publications were never a threat to the security of the state, nor were they ever considered more than "interesting if impractical" by the authorities. An early article he wrote on "The Continental Triumvirate and Perpetual Peace" for the *Bulletin de Lyon* (17 December 1803) attracted Napoleon's attention. He caused inquiries to be made, and Ballanche, the editor, in reply, wrote that Fourier ". . . [est] un homme modeste, étranger à toute espèce d'ambition et jouissant parmi nous autres, jeunes hommes de ce temps, d'une grande réputation de science géographique".[27] His suggestions and ideas were ignored, but an offer of employment in the Ministry of Foreign Affairs was made, only to be declined by the independent Fourier. Much later, during the Hundred Days, Fourier was however to accept from his distant cousin Baron Fourier[28] the post of Head of the Bureau of Statistics of the Rhône Prefecture.[29]

From his earliest years, Fourier developed a keen interest in geography, music and botany. He would spend whole nights poring over maps and atlases he had bought with his pocket money.[30] As a child too, he had learnt the pleasures of cultivating flowers. His bedroom was his greenhouse, and there he grew varied species.³¹ Music he learnt almost alone and without masters. He was well versed in the theory of music, played several instruments and composed.³² He was to remain passionately devoted to these pursuits—studying them keenly and methodically for the remainder of his life. Later he was to produce a new method of musical notation, which it was said "singularly facilitates the reading of music and suppresses the complication resulting from plurality of keys".³³

Fourier never married and as is the wont with many bachelors he appreciated good living and loved animals, especially cats "avec une sollicitude toute paternelle".³⁴ A friend of Brillat-Savarin, he had developed decided opinions and views on cooking. Such was his aversion to bread "mal cuit" and adulterated wine ("les vins frelatés") that he took his own bread and wine when he visited certain restaurants.³⁵ He had no liking for 'a cup of tea'. "C'est encore l'anglomanie", he said, speaking of the Parisians³⁶ "qui les a habitués à proscrire au déjeuner les bons mets de leur pays et à les remplacer par une vilenie qu'on appelle thé, drogue dont les Anglais s'accomodent forcément, parce qu'ils n'ont ni bon vins, ni bons fruits, à moins d'énorme dépenses. Ils sont réduits au thé comme les malades, et au beurre comme les enfants." His keen interest and pleasure in good well-cooked food had, as we shall see, a big influence on the shape of his educational doctrine.³⁷

Fourier, with his natural sensitivity, his love of order, his desire for justice and his natural benevolence, was early outraged by the events around him. He could see no need for and no end to the perpetual struggle for personal wealth and self-aggrandizement. Deliberate lying, particularly for monetary gain, disgusted him.

Not content with mere criticism and lamentation, Fourier long brooded upon the reasons for human exploitation and brutality, the stupid waste of effort and resources, the co-existence of frustration and helpless poverty side by side with ill-gotten wealth. All this he saw daily clearly around him. While in the cavalry, he had devised a plan to end profiteering in the Army;³⁸ but his plans necessitated drastic changes in organization and were consequently not acceptable to the Directory. In 1799, while employed in Marseilles, he was involved in an episode which was to leave a deep impression on him. Sacks of rice were thrown into the sea to keep the price at a profitable level rather than be sold to an impoverished populace at a loss.[39] Struck by all these hatreds and wastes, he had an ardent desire to end them.[40] Fourier considered himself an inventor of genius. "La nature donne à chacun le sien. Elle partage les talents: le mien est celui d'inventeur."[41] One of the clues that had led him to the discovery of the Theory of Attraction, was the sale of apples in Paris at about ten times the price they were then being sold at elsewhere.[42] This caused him to realize that there was something radically wrong with the economic system. He was proud that an apple should have started him upon his discoveries, in the same way as the apple had revealed the law of gravity to Newton, for he claimed to be a second Newton but working in the moral and social sciences. "La théorie de l'attraction passionnée est la continuation du calcul de Newton."[43]

Fourier was firmly convinced of his mission in life, for he believed that God had willed . . . "que le Théorie du Mouvement Universal échût en partage à un homme presque illitéré. C'est un sergent de boutique qui va confondre ces bibliothèques politiques et morales, fruit honteux des charlataneries antiques et modernes. Eh! ce n'est pas la première fois que Dieu se sert de l'humble pour abaisser le superbe, et qu'il fait choix de l'homme le plus obscur pour apporter au monde le plus important message."[44] But industrious and keen though he was, progress was slow. "Entre temps il est bon de rappeler que depuis l'an 1799, où je trouvai le germe du calcul de l'attraction, j'ai toujours été absorbé par mes occupations mercantiles, et pouvant à peine donner quelques instants aux problèmes passionnels dont souvent un seul exige des recherches soutenues pendant plusieurs années. Aprés avoir employé mes journées à servir les fourberies des marchands, et m'hébeter ou abrutir dans les fonctions mensongères et avilissantes, je ne pouvais pas employer les nuits à m'initier aux sciences vraies pour en faire l'application à ma théorie passionnelle. Je suis obligé d'abandonner cette magnifique proie, la théorie de l'application, aux savants des classes fixes. Qu'ils s'applaudissent de ce que la fortune m'a mal servi, leur part sera d'autant plus belle!"[45]

Yet surprisingly, Fourier wrote an astonishing amount; he wrote regularly, so many pages a day, and altogether produced a dozen weighty volumes. His first book, published when he was thirty-six, the *Théorie des Quatres Mouvements* (1808)[46] contained a preliminary sketch of his ideas. Fourteen years later he worked these out in greater detail when he brought out his *Traité de l'Association Domestique-Agricole* (1822, 2 vols.) later reprinted as *La Théorie de l'Unité Universelle* in four volumes. This is his major work, in which education is discussed at considerable length. After this Fourier attempted to provide a summary of his opinions in *Le Nouveau Monde Industriel et Sociétaire* (1829). Finally in *La Fausse Industrie* (1835-6, 2 vols.), he gathered together a miscellaneous collection of essays and jottings. After his death his disciples published his Manuscripts (1851-8, 4 vols.), which represent however only a part of the papers he left.[47]

Fourier wrote on several topics at the same time, following his inclinations and interests. He was thus carrying out his own precept of alternative labour; but "Quand j'ai un problème en tête", he wrote,[48] "j'ai l'habitude de laisser toutes mes lettres en arrière, je renvoie toute autre affaire jusqu'à ce qu'il soit résolu". He wrote on a vast variety of subjects: cosmology, psychology, social and political economy, historical and metaphysical philosophy, commerce, politics and morals, as well as specifically on education. He treated them all as part of one general system of nature; united by one universal law—the law of movement.[49]

Fourier's books are difficult[50] and are written by a man ignorant of the art of writing.[51] Fourier is aware of this deficiency and warns the reader that "On trouvera dans le cours de l'ouvrage et des notes subséquentes divers tableaux dont la nomenclature pourra sembler impropre et mal choisie, car je possède fort peu la language française. Il faudra donc s'attacher aux idées plus qu'aux mots, sur le choix desquels j'avoue mon insuffisance. A cet égard, j'adopterai des nomenclatures plus correctes quand elles me seront communiquées." Replying to a reviewer in *La Revue française,* Fourier wrote "mon style est celui d'un homme qui n'a pas de prétension au fauteuil, et qui va droit au but sans patelinage académique . . ."[52] Fourier was essentially a thinker, visionary and reformer. His style, as one of his English admirers, the Rev. John Morell, explained, "was not of a kind calculated to make a book sell, sinewy, pithy, and somewhat careless in appearance, it was not adapted to please many readers".[53] He loved inventing new words, was constantly finding improvements, and so making his ideas all the more difficult to follow. "No other reformer was as bold and prolific an innovator in language as Fourier."[54] Many of Fourier's wild notions and mad exaggerations have made him an easy prey for ridicule, and yet, are they as fantastic as they seemed one hundred and fifty years ago? Man's life prolonged to a hundred and forty-four years "on an average"; the oceans transformed into seas of lemonade; lions and sharks making way for "anti-lions" and "anti-sharks" of a very domestic nature; the Pole warmed and rendered fertile by a new aurora borealis; the dexterity of our toes sufficiently practised to play the piano; a simple operation "dans les ventricules du coeur" to enable man to be equally at home in land and sea; satellites round the earth to light up our dark nights; our planets enriched by four satellites; interplanetary communications . . .[55] It is his form of presentation that is perhaps absurd. And this absurdity is heightened by Fourier's individual and peculiar style. He was, moreover, credited with a greater amount of eccentricity than he actually possessed for few had actually read his work.[56] Nevertheless, allowing for these idiosyncrasies of style, and ignoring some of his more fanciful ideas, one cannot help but be attracted by the charm and genius of this extraordinary man. "Owen and Fourier", wrote J. S. Mill in his *Autobiography*,[57] "have entitled themselves to the grateful remembrance of future generations." But Fourier's intellectual work, when taken as a whole, though more Utopian and less restrained in character than Owen's, has (according to Charles Gide) "a considerably wider outlook, and combines the keenest appreciation of the evils of civilization with an almost uncanny power of divining the future".[58]

Like most inventors of Utopias Fourier had hoped that once his theory had been revealed to the world its acceptance and implementation would follow as a matter of course, espoused perhaps by a rich and powerful patron, as Columbus' discovery of America was made possible through the help of Isabella of Castille. "Je veux", he used to say, "faire de nouvelles tentatives pour trouver un protecteur à notre affaire. Tous les petits clients, les menus partisans, ne servent à rien et sont difficiles à diriger. Il faudrait en trouver un grand qui ferait plus à lui seul que cent mille pygmées."[59] For the last ten years of his life, which he spent almost entirely in Paris, he would return home at noon, for this was the hour he had set for interview with prospective patrons.[60]

Like all Utopians he was to find most men indifferent or even positively hostile to his plans for the amelioration of their lot. His *Théorie des Quatres Mouvements* hardly attracted attention.[61] Recognition was very slow, and he always experienced much difficulty in publishing his works.[62] He met his first disciple, Jules Muiron, in 1816,[63] but it was not until the 1830s, in the last years of his life, that his work began to attract wide public interest[64] and gather a sizable following. In June 1832 his admirers started publishing a weekly journal, *Le Phalanstère*, later renamed *La Réforme Industrielle*, to propagate his ideas and it found over a thousand subscribers. Books were also written about him, notably Victor Considérant's *Destinée Sociale* (1834), perhaps the most intelligent and coherent exposition of the master's doctrines.[65] Fourierism also began to be discussed in the press, and particularly the provincial press, while Pope Gregory XVI put the *Nouveau Monde* and the *Destinée Sociale* on the Index.[66]

As his fame grew and he became almost a celebrity, so it became more fashionable to hear him discuss his own theories and have him to dinner. Fourier, always jealous of his independence, accepted only when he knew his hosts sufficiently well and felt that the furtherance of his cause would benefit, and then he only rarely went out of his way to ingratiate himself with the assembled company.[67]

Those who met him did not easily forget him. Proudhon, who as a printer had supervized the production of the *Nouveau Monde* in 1829, had several opportunities of talking with Fourier. "I knew Fourier. He had a medium-sized head, wide shoulders and chest, a nervous carriage, narrow brow, mediocre cranium; a certain air of enthusiasm which spread over his face gave him the look of an ecstatic dilettante . . . For six whole weeks I was the captive of this bizarre genius."[68] Different though their theories were on many points, nevertheless Fourier had a lasting influence and effect on Proudhon's philosophical, social and educational[69] beliefs. Sir Alexander

Gray,[70] hardly a fellow traveller or lover of socialism, is "spiritually, despite or because of their absurdities" much more at home with Saint-Simon and Fourier than Marx. While Sir Alexander "would do much to avoid meeting Marx—for this Diotrephes of the socialist church would merely bark at me in his hot displeasure—I should greatly appreciate a long evening with Fourier in a quiet hostelry; and if the bar were not too crowded, I believe I could prevail upon him to give his marvellous impersonation of a fox or a robin or a giraffe, with copious comments on the qualities each of them symbolized. It was a performance which he gave only when his company was entirely congenial."[71] Whenever he felt that the company had come to meet him purely out of idle curiosity he would become sullen and would only answer persistent questions. He could, however, be the most talkative and stimulating companion.

He became better known after his death. The Fourierist school expanded further, its influence widened[72] and spread outside France. No other early school of socialists has had such an immense literature,[73] and yet none has had less attention from students of education.

Fourier always claimed that his theories were absolutely new[74] and owed nothing to book learning. When he quoted the work of others, it was usually to show that they agreed with him! As a young man he had read a great deal. He was fond of poetry and especially admired Molière and La Fontaine.[75] Voltaire, too, he esteemed, but criticized for having failed to see that his ideas should have led him to the discovery of the Laws of Attraction.[76] But Fourier had no deep, real or detailed knowledge of Montesquieu, Rousseau, Voltaire and Condillac. He himself admits once having started reading Condillac only to give up after a few pages: "Ces ouvrages de métaphysique m'ennuient si fort qu'ayant un jour commencé la lecture du phénix de la science, du divin Condillac, je ne pus arriver au bout du deuxième chapitre."[77] He also boasted that he had never read John Locke.[78] However, he had come across these and many more mainly in discussion and in the secondary sources, pamphlets and newspapers, that he perused in the various reading rooms,[79] and, for the last ten years of his life, at the Palais-Royal.[80] He had, for example, followed the work of Pestalozzi with keen interest in the columns of the *Moniteur*.[81]

The nature of Fourier's thought, his own reticence to acknowledge himself heir to any previous thinker, makes it difficult to trace his intellectual origins precisely. As Professor J. Zilberfarb has indicated, these origins remain somewhat obscure.[82] Nevertheless, it is still possible to discern important influences upon his intellectual development. He discussed and criticized the ideas of Saint-Simon and his followers without, it seems, having actually read any of their original works.[83] The influence of Robert Owen is more likely. Owen's work had been described by H. G. Macnab in 1819[84] and this book was translated by Laffon de Labebat into French in 1821. Labebat's translation was extensively reviewed and discussed in the papers.[85] Moreover, the fact that Fourier had hardly discussed education in his *Théorie des Quatre Mouvements* published in 1808, but in 1822 had done so in his *Traité de l'Association* . . . , may mean that he was influenced by Owen; but this must remain an hypothesis. Professor William Brickman claims that it was Robert Owen who received his inspiration from Fourier,[86] but he does not give supporting evidence.

Dr. Johnes likewise maintains that Saint-Simon and Fourier, although of the same progressive school of thought, nevertheless belong to different streams. "Saint-Simon was heir to the traditional theory of progress, regarding Condorcet as one of his precursors. Fourier was heir to that other stream of progress in the eighteenth century stemming from Mably, Morelly, Rousseau, in which the essential contention was that man, while progressive by nature, had travelled the wrong road in reaching the existing state of civilization.[87] Indeed Fourier uses the words "civilized" and "civilization" in the same derogatory manner as the Marxists now use the terms capitalist and capitalism to describe western society.

It is however useless to seek any carefully worked out, rigorous and academically 'respectable' philosophical basis for Fourier's proposals. Nevertheless, as Professor Dautry has pointed out, Fourier was fairly well acquainted with the general ideas of Condillac and Rousseau.[88] The ideas of these men permeated the atmosphere of the period. There is no reason to disbelieve Fourier's claim that he had never read them in the original. He picked them up unconsciously and naturally at second hand. "When however a system of philosophy attains wide currency as to be familiar to people who have never read the books or seen it in practice, it may safely be assumed that it has shed many of its riches on the way, and that the only operative part remaining is that essential core which has been permanently incorporated into the human heritage."[89] Fourier was a critic and disciple of his age, a commentator on the morals of his time, a visionary and extreme optimist who saw the possibility of happiness for all. He was a common man's philosopher, but on a much lower level than his contemporaries, e.g. Condorcet and perhaps Saint-Simon. But despite this, or because of it, he was perhaps better able to understand the simple aspirations and desires of the ordinary man.

1. In his first work, *La Théorie des Quatre Mouvements*, Fourier wrote his name with two R's, but in all his other writings he adopted the orthography now known.
2. Charles Pellarin, *Fourier, Sa Vie et Sa Théorie* (1871, 5th ed.), 28. Pellarin's work seems to be the basis of all subsequent biographical work on the life of Fourier. See e.g. A. Guillot, *C. Fourier, Almanack Social pour l'Année 1840*; Jean Czinski, *Notice biographique sur Charles Fourier* (1841).
3. Ibid., 28.
4. Ibid., 29.
5. Ibid., 67.
6. Ibid., 48.
7. Ibid., 37 and 72.
8. 1775–1826. French politician and writer. Fled to Switzerland during the Terror (1792) and to U.S. (1793). Returned to Paris (1796); judge of Court of Cassation during Consulate. Best known for his *Physiologie du Goût* (1825).
9. Pellarin, op. cit., 36.
10. Ibid., 45.
11. Ibid., 27.
12. "Sur cette éducation, sur cette formation, nous n'avons d'autres témoignages que ceux que nous trouvons dans son oeuvre." H. Bourgin, *Fourier* (1905), 41. See also S. Droz, *Histoire du Collège de Besançon*, 2 vols. (1868); L. Borne, *L'instruction Populaire en Franche-Comté avant 1792*, 2 vols. (1949).
13. Bourgin, op. cit., 31.
14. Ibid., 32.
15. Pellarin, op. cit., 32–3. The other two Laureats of his class, the only ones mentioned with him, were J. B. Couchery, who was recording secretary of the Chamber of Deputies in the first years of the Restoration; and J. J. Ordinaire, who later became Rector of the Academy at Besançon. Fourier's most intimate college friend was Ordinaire, and their friendship lasted a

long while. Ordinaire, though he never accepted Fourier's theories, neverthless always held his childhood friend in high regard. He was always to speak highly of Fourier's aptitude for the arts and sciences, and his astonishing intellectual capacity.

16. Pellarin, op. cit., 31.
17. 1565–1640. Roman Catholic priest, founder (1597) of the religious order of School sisters of Notre Dame; see also L. Borne, *L'Instruction pupulaire en Franche-Comté avant 1792* (1949); J. Renault, *Les Idées pédagogiques de Saint Pierre Fourier* (1919); M. Cord'homme, *Un Educateur du seizième siècle, saint Pierre Fourier* (1932). Nevertheless Charles was not, as far as it can be ascertained, indebted to his famous ancestor.
18. Pellarin, op. cit., 36.
19. Ibid., 37.
20. Ibid., 38.
21. Ibid., 91.
22. Ibid., 38.
23. Ibid., 43.
24. Ibid., 45.
25. 23 August 1793. Decree of National Convention.
26. Pellarin, op. cit., 49.
27. Ibid., 55.
28. Jean Baptiste Joseph Fourier, 1768–1830. Mathematician and physicist. Remembered chiefly for his "Fourier Series". See any book on Calculus or Analysis. Probably influenced Charles Fourier's "Series". (See Chapter 2.)
29. Pellarin, op. cit., 64.
30. Ibid., 32.
31. Ibid., 32.
32. Ibid., 33.
33. See also *Fausse Industrie*, Vol. 2, 528.
34. Ibid., 183.
35. Ibid., 157.
36. N. M., 300.
37. U. U., iv, 104, 79, 76.
38. Ibid., 50.
39. Ibid., 51.
40. Ibid., 43.
41. Quoted ibid., 93.
42. Ibid., 41; Cp. Manus. (1951), 17.
43. N. M., 161. Cp. "Newton a pris l'initiative en calcul de l'attraction, que [Fourier] a étendu au mouvement passionnel." See N. M., 3, 25, 156, 160, 322.
44. Q. M., 152.
45. Manus. (1851), 23.
46. These four movements refer to the four basic factors of life—social, animal, organic and material. The rather obscure meaning of this is explained in Q. M., 29–30.
47. For a complete bibliography of Fourier's works see G. Del Bo, *Il*

Socialismo Utopistico. I. Charles Fourier e la Scuola Societaria (1801–1922), Milano, 1957. For a review of the more recent post-1945 work on Fourier and Fourierism see Professor J. Zilberfarb's articles "Post-war Foreign literature on Fourier and Fourierism" (in Russian) in *Istoriya sotsialisticheskikh uchenii* (History of Socialist teaching—collected essays) (1962), 438–63.

48. Quoted by Pellarin, op. cit., 143, from a letter to his friend Muiron 20 February 1818.
49. Cp. H. Doherty, *Introduction to "The Passions of the Human Soul"* (1851), v.
50. Bourgin, op. cit., 155.
51. Ibid., 155.
52. Quoted by Pellarin, op. cit., 102.
53. J. R. Morell, *Sketch of life of Charles Fourier* (1849), 13. One is reminded of Buffon's epigram "Le style c'est l'homme".
54. A. E. Bestor, "Evolution of Socialist Vocabulary", *Journal of the History of Ideas* (June 1948), 283.
55. C. Gide, *Les Prophéties de Fourier* (1894), 4, etc.
56. Gide and Rist, op. cit., 255.
57. *Autobiography* (1873), 168.
58. Gide and Rist, op. cit., 255.
59. Quoted by Pellarin, op. cit., 129.
60. Ibid., 146. Daudet-Dulany attempted to set up a phalanstère at Condé, but this effort was doomed to failure because of lack of capital. Fourier soon dissociated himself from this enterprise for the founders were hardly following his principles and it soon disintegrated.
61. Ibid., 62; also Bourgin, op. cit., 156.
62. Ibid., 96–7.
63. Ibid., 64.
64. M. Friedberg, *L'Influence de Charles Fourier*, 9.
65. Victor Prosper Considerant (1809–1893), born Salins. Leader of Fourierists (from 1837). See e.g. C. Coignet, *Victor Considerant, Sa Vie, Son Oeuvre* (1895); H. Bourgin, *Victor Considerant, Son Oeuvre* (1909); P. Louis, *Histoire du Socialisme en France* (1925).
66. Friedberg, op. cit., 10; also *Index Librorum Prohibitorum* (1948), 107, 177.
67. Pellarin, op. cit., 124.
68. Quoted by G. Woodcock, *Proudhon, A Biography* (1956), 13.
69. "Sur Proudhon aussi, la pensée de Fourier a sans doute fait une grande impression. Il s'agit, disait-il dans la *Capacité Politique*, de développer, par une éducation intégrale, comme disait Fourier, le plus grand nombre d'aptitudes et de créer la plus grande capacité possibles." (Ed. Rivière, 1924, 345)—M. Friedberg, *L'Influence de Charles Fourier sur le Mouvement Social contemporain en France* (1926), 71.
70. Sometime Professor of Political Economy, Edinburgh University.
71. *The Socialist Tradition*, v.
72. See H. Friedberg, op. cit.; also G. D. H. Cole, "As varieties of his terminology were endless; so too Fourier's disciples were called and called themselves by a similar diversity of names." Op. cit., 71.
73. Bourgin, op. cit., 422; Lansac, op. cit., 25.

74. Bourgin, op. cit., 60.
75. Pellarin, op. cit., 142.
76. Ibid., 141. Also N. M., 355.
77. Quoted Bourgin, op. cit., 61; Manus. (1851), 13.
78. Q. M., 285; Manus. (1851), 33.
79. Bourgin, op. cit., 65–7.
80. Pellarin, op. cit., 142.
81. Bourgin, op. cit., 62.
82. J. Zilberfarb, "Les Etudes sur Fourier et le Fourierisme", in *Revue Internationale de Philosophie*, No. 60, Fasc. 2 (1962), 275. See also his "Sources for a study of the ideological heritage of Charles Fourier", in *Novyy i noveyshiy istoriya* No. 1 (1963), 122–130.
83. Bourgin, *Etudes sur les sources de Fourier* (1905), 57.
84. H. G. Macnab, *The New views of Mr. Owen of Lanark . . . also observations of the New Lanark School, and of the Systems of Education of Mr. Owen, of the Rev. Dr. Bell, and that of the New British and Foreign System of Mutual Instruction*, London, 1819.
85. H. Bourgin, op. cit., 61.
86. *The Changing Soviet School*, edited by G. Z. F. Bereday, et al. (1960), 56.
87. M. H. Johnes, *Influence of the Philosophy of Progress on French Educational Theory and Practice from 1789–1848*, Ph.D. Thesis, Wales, 1952.
88. J. Dautry, "Fourier et les Questions d'éducation", in *Revue Internationale de Philosophie*, No. 60. Fasc. 2. (1962), 234–5.
89. P. Hazard, *The European Mind 1680–1715* (1953), 131.

CHAPTER TWO

The Psychological Basis of Fourier's Educational Thought

FOURIER's educational ideas, as well as his political schemes, are based on a psychological theory. His originality as a socialist, and his importance as an educationalist, derive from his being interested not only in realizing abstract principles of justice, but in understanding human nature. He starts from an investigation of the nature of man, he analyses man's inclinations, capacities and needs, and from this he proceeds to deduce a social order that will fully employ all his capacities and satisfy all his needs.[1]

Fourier considered that the world in which he lived was "an abyss of misery, falsehood, stupidities, injustices, and oppressions". It had been for three thousand years "the kingdom of Satan and Moloch"[2] because men had failed to study nature's ways and so had never tried to organize society in accordance with the laws of nature.[3] A few geniuses, like Socrates, Voltaire, Montesquieu and Rousseau,[4] had come near to discovering these laws but they had not actually been successful and nothing had come of their efforts.[5] Political and moral sciences, Fourier says, have done nothing to improve human happiness in the course of twenty-five centuries,[6] above all because they have tried only to "*alter* the nature of man, to extinguish forces in the soul, under the pretext that they do not suit the social order, instead of seeking a social order appropriate to the nature of man".[7] It was essential, in his view, to discard all previous moral theories, to construct a new one based on "experimental truth"[8] and strictly in accordance with 'nature'.[9]

Fourier is a believer in the existence of God, not in a particularly religious sense, but rather as some mysterious life force which gives direction and impetus to the spiritual and material universe.[10] The actions and ends of God, or of this force, are neither arbitrary, nor are they aimless. God, the eternal Geometer, does not proceed arbitrarily: everything is determined by fixed laws.[11] Fourier sees the whole of creation as one complete unit. Nature for him is God, the Universe and man,[12] all that is governed by fixed rules, for God follows his own rules. The problem therefore is to discover the laws, and to establish a system in accordance with them.

Fourier discovers these laws by "analogy".[13] He quotes Schelling to the effect that the world is constructed on the model of the human soul and that the same principles are to be found in every part of the Universe, in perfect analogy.[14] It is a simple matter therefore to proceed from the known to the unknown.[15]

The physical world, as Newton discovered, is ruled by the force of gravity. Transposing this into human terms (by analogy) Fourier claims that the corresponding force which rules men is 'attraction'.[16] This attraction—more fully "attraction passionnelle ou passionnée"—is the driving power (moteur) in man, the "active principle" of nature.

This 'attraction' manifests itself in human beings through their passions. Fourier uses the term 'passion' analogously with 'mass' in mechanics, when most would think of 'weight'. Whereas gravity acts on mass to produce a force or weight; similarly, in human terms, 'attraction' acts on the 'passions', to produce 'social activity'. 'Attraction' is the motivator or life force which "triggers off", stimulates, or directs the passions.[17]

Fourier defines 'attraction' as consisting of twelve passions,[18] which men possess in varying degrees of intensity. Five *sensitive* passions are concerned with the satisfaction of the five senses.[19] Four *affective* passions influence men's relations with others—namely, their family, their friendships, their sex life and their ambitions.[20] The three *distributive* passions—rivalry, boredom and enthusiasm—modify the exercise of the other passions. These distributive passions perhaps need further explanation.

Fourier sees the distributive passions as elements or components of basic behaviour or as three broad needs. Man, he believes, is driven, in varying degrees and at different times, towards the manifestation of these three distributive types of behaviour as he tends to organize himself into the four basic affective groups. First, Fourier asserts, man is quarrelsome by nature, and so needs for his happiness and satisfaction opportunities for argument, dispute, rivalry and competition.[21] Indeed, Fourier believes that it is not God's wish that men should conform nor that they should live quiet and docile lives.[22] Rather God has rendered us most strongly inclined towards rivalry and intrigue: if His wishes had been otherwise, He would have, according to Fourier, rendered men "molles et apathiques".[23] Secondly, man has a craving for variety in life, for frequent change of occupation, the "manie de voltiger d'un plaisir à l'autre".[24] Thirdly, man has a craving for 'blind enthusiasm', the desire for excess, the wish to abandon moderation, the need for the assertion of the romantic.

Fourier's whole system is designed to give satisfaction to these twelve passions "as nature has given them to man, without changing anything in them and believing that what God has created He created well".[25] In the world as it is, these passions conflict to produce discord. However, Fourier's analysis of them points the way to eliminating this conflict.[26] He shows that there are three distinct problems:[27] the satisfaction of the five senses; the gratification of the individual's desire for human links; and the adjustment of these passions to enhance them and to prevent them conflicting. The last aim, the fulfilment of the distributive passions, is thus crucial, and it alone makes the others possible.

The means Fourier invents to achieve all three aims is the phalange, which in modern terms could be described as a group theory. Fourier had carefully calculated that the ideal community—the phalange or phalanstère—should be one of approximately eighteen hundred men, women and children. This optimum size, he maintained, would enable all its members, freely and spontaneously, to express their desires and their potentialities, collectively organized in a series of groups. There would be no repression of any desires or talents. Men, according to Fourier, are born with varied tastes, talents, unequal abilities. Men, in fact, are by instinct enemies of equality; and moreover, their inequalities are essential and need to be cultivated.[28] Once developed, Fourier optimistically asserts, they will harmoniously interact within the groups of the phalange.

For Fourier, therefore, education must be collectively organized in groups, because it is within these groups that the passions can best find fulfilment. A valuable feature of his thought is that he not only concentrates on the individual, but also on the individual in society. His system is therefore designed to enable the individual, while fully satisfying his personal needs, to integrate himself in his society.[29]

The cultivation of the basic senses—taste, sight, touch, smell, hearing—is fundamental and, as we shall later see in detail, Fourier devises ingenious and original methods for their development. The affective passions, because their utilization leads to the formation of groups are one reason for Fourier's insistence on collective education. The passions for friendship and sex are, says Fourier, particularly powerful between ten to fifteen years[30] and fifteen to twenty years respectively, and so he utilized these in his schemes. The distributive passions, however, furnish the rules which guide the behaviour of all in the phalange and so govern educational procedure. Fourier wishes that the education of the child be integrated and balanced. He recognizes that the various aspects of the child's physical and mental personality mature at different stages and rates. But unlike Rousseau, Fourier does not draw a sharp line between the stages, nor does he forget that the child's life is one continuous development.[31] Fourier sees the need to develop both body and mind simultaneously;[33] but he does make the proviso that the former ought to preoccupy but not dominate the first ten years of a child's life; and vice versa in the next ten years.[34]

The first ten years are thus primarily, though not exclusively, concerned with the material aspects of education: the child's bodily vigour and manual dexterity are developed, his talents discovered and their training taken in hand. In his teens, his propensity for friendship is exploited and diverted into socially useful occupations;[34] likewise later, his sexual desires will be sublimated (for a while at any rate) into work, appropriate to his age and developed skill.[35]

A criticism of Fourier's work from the point of view of our present day experimentally based child psychology is both unnecessary and futile. Modern educational psychology is based upon scientific and statistically rigorous techniques, whereas Fourier's psychological conclusions were formed upon his personal observation and reflection. Even merely as a 'common sense' description of man's desires and urges, Fourier's account is highly exaggerated and one-sided. There are too many omissions: thinking and intelligence, memory and abstraction are but a few topics which receive little or almost no attention. Nevertheless, he has his merits. He appreciated the child as a person, as an individual with certain needs and appetites which require satisfaction for his fulfilment, development and growth. In his educational proposals, he seeks to provide these for all children, irrespective of class; and in so doing he foreshadows, albeit in a rudimentary way, the work of modern educational psychology.

Fourier devotes considerable space to the analysis of groups. The principal characteristic of a group, says Fourier, is a common aim. He appreciates that a group can be a mere assembly of persons intent merely on passing the time "réunis par ennui, sans passions, sans but", or congregated together for some other equally frivolous or subversive purpose. But in his theory of passions he defines a group as "une masse lignée par identité de goût pour une fonction exercée".[36] In Fourier's groups the members must have identity of interest and purpose and must be intent on accomplishing some clearly defined task: such as removing the weeds from the onion patch, or making stools in the workshops, or peeling potatoes in the kitchens. The various groups associated with onion cultivation would form a 'series'; likewise the stool makers would belong to the carpentry series. The group in the phalange is thus a functional unit, purposefully but freely and spontaneously organized with a clear, coherent aim in view.

The members of any group ought to be linked "par une ou plusieurs affections communes",[37] and the relations must never become embittered, hypocritical or destructive. Discord and competition must be confined to inter-group rivalry.[38] The maintenance of internal group harmony and the confinement of hostility and rivalry towards competitors necessitates that the abilities and talents of the group's members are very carefully graded and fully used in the group work. Each individual member will feel that he is contributing and giving of his best only so long as he knows that his talents are, in fact, fully developed and trained, or in the process of becoming so. Fourier sees no reason why persons of different skills should not work together and feel equally satisfied. Not all within any group will have equal talent, nor equally developed skill; indeed, some groups for effective functioning will need similar skills variously developed. However, individuals in the process of developing their skill will welcome the opportunity of work alongside skilled craftsmen. Indeed, as we shall see, emulation and example are an important method of training in the phalange.

The members of most groups will differ widely in age, aptitude and ability, and will be drawn from the ranks of men, women or children. Where necessary individuals will thus come, freely and spontaneously, to form a group in the pursuit of a common aim. As soon as differences of talent and purpose arise and free association becomes impossible, new groups would form in competition and rivalry with existing ones. This constant group rivalry would involve much activity, planning and discussion, scheming for advantage, and a general attempt to surpass standards attained by others, and so give ample opportunity for the exercise of "the mania for intrigue".

Inter-group rivalry will be, however, insufficient by itself "pour électriser les groupes dans leurs travaux".[39] It is necessary, argues Fourier, to augment this rivalry, with "blind enthusiasm", i.e. combine careful reflection and scheming with inspiration and romantic notions.[40] This, evoking as it will the pleasures of the senses and of the mind, will engender enthusiasm for the task in hand and make it easier for the attainment of the aim or the surmounting of the obstacles.

In civilization, the passion for constant change of occupation, the "butterfly" instinct, as Fourier calls it, is regarded as and is termed a vice,[41] but this he argues is not as God intended it to be. The twelve to fifteen hour stints worked in civilization, without diversion and exclusively at one basic operation, would indeed be pleasant and satisfying if "Dieu nous aurait donné le goût de la monotonie, l'horreur de la variété". In Fourier's opinion, the reverse is true, and so sessions ought to be short and should not exceed one and a half hours. The associative passion, formidable though it is, cannot engender enthusiasm for a very long period, and so "Dieu par convenance à cet ordre industriel, a dû nous donner la passion de papillonage, le besoin de variété fréquenté dans les occupations".[42] Likewise, God has also given each individual some twenty different talents, and once these have been discovered and developed, the individual will be able to indulge his fancy and move from one occupation to another throughout the day.[43]

F. Zweig, well known for his surveys of working-class life, is aware of the "butterfly principle" conceived by Fourier, but he writes that "no such scheme it seems from my survey would be acceptable or even conceivable to British workers. Once they are settled in a job and like it, they prefer to stay put for their whole lifetime. True, they like variety, and this was frequently mentioned to me, whenever I asked what is it they liked mostly in the job, but they mean variety in the job in which they have settled, and not outside it. They like 'something new to learn' (this was also frequently mentioned), but it must be within their compass, in the framework of what they already know, not outside it."[44]

Fourier constantly emphasizes that harmonization within the group can hardly occur unless three conditions are fulfilled: the association must be free of compulsory ties, or of obligations beyond those of decorum; all members must have a blind passion for the branch of industry or kind of pleasure common to the group; and devotion to the interest of the group must be boundless with no counting of the cost for the maintenance of the common interest.[45]

Freedom and spontaneous activity are hardly compatible with the tenets of an orderly and harmonious society, hence Fourier is at great pains to emphasize the importance of the early discovery of talent and vocation, and the education of children, so that all might partake fully in the life of the community.[46] This early "natural" education will prevent subsequent disequilibrium, neurosis, maladjustment and frustration of the individual with himself, with his entourage, as well as with God.[47]

Fourier attempts the development of a mathematical theory of group formation, believing as he does that "les mathématiques sont l'arbitre éternel de la justice dans toutes les oeuvres de Dieu".[48] His theory however is a bizarre one, being based on analogy from musical notation. Indeed it is scarcely comprehensible and certainly it is not mathematically rigorous or analytical. His mathematical knowledge was not adequate nor were the mathematical techniques of his time sufficiently developed. Lack of time and knowledge, Fourier claims, forced him to leave this development to others: "C'est un beau fleuron que je leur abandonne, je leur jalouse une découverte dont ils trouveront le germe dans la théorie des passions. Si j'avais une année pleine à donner à cette [travail] je ne l'aurais pas laissée aux géomètres."[49]

Certainly the work of Kepler,[50] Baron Fourier and other mathematicians supplied our Fourier with his terminology.[51] The attempt to give mathematical precision to the ways of nature was nothing new. "Le bon sens réduit au calcul" (Laplace). The Greeks had attempted to interpret truth, beauty, and the laws of nature in mathematical terms. Fontenelle, in his "Eloge de Montmort", had declared "Le monde politique, aussi bien que le physique, se règle par poids, nombre et mesure".[52] Condorcet in his "*Tableau général de la science* . . ." had written "La science ne peut faire de progrès qu'autant qu'elle sera cultivée par des géomètres qui auront approfondi les sciences sociales".[53] Fourier wrote: "Il doit exister une théorie d'harmonie géometrique pour le monde social, comme pour le monde matériel, et il faut recourir à une politique sociale calquée sur la théorie newtonienne d'équilibre matériel de l'univers . . ."[54]

Although Fourier fails to evolve a coherent mathematical theory, nevertheless, he must be considered as a scientific precursor in the study of ergonometrics and group theory.[55] Fourier was perhaps the first consciously to realize and advocate the need for a study of small groups as a guide to the understanding of social behaviour, and the imperative necessity for foresight and planning in the establishment of harmonious and fruitful relations in industry as well as in educational institutions. It is only comparatively recently that the scientific study of these difficult problems has begun.[56]

In education he is a pioneer in advocating and developing the theory of group learning. True, he knew but disapproved of the mutual teaching system first advocated by Lancaster and Bell, "récemment établit en Europe, avec tel succès".[57] His conception of group learning is wider, and inevitably similar projects were developed independently at a later date. The collectivist tendency of Fourier's theory make his schemes strikingly similar to many educational methods in Soviet pedagogy. Many of his principles have been partially adopted, if not generally accepted, in the most surprising quarters: Boy Scouts, 'play-way', individual work schemes, project methods, group activities, the Dalton Plan, and similar variants.

1. Cp. M. Buber, op. cit., 11.
2. U. U., i, 52, 177; N. M., 366.
3. U. U., ii, 189.
4. U. U., ii, 50.
5. N. M., 355, 368.
6. Q. M., 23. For the "Fausseté et insuffisance de nos lumières sociales et politiques" see U. U., ii, 109 etc. Also U. U., ii, 54. Cp. Q. M., 409.
7. U. U., ii, 118 (Fourier's italics.)
8. On the "devoirs d'étude méthodique", see U. U., ii, 130–40.
9. "Back to nature was at the time a rallying cry", see H. Nicolson, *The Age of Reason* (1960), 399 etc.
10. Q. M., 46; also U. U., ii, 265.
11. U. U., iv, 470.
12. "Dieu, l'univers, l'homme, sont identiques, le type de cette trinité est Dieu. Le mouvement est en analogie avec Dieu." N. M., 445.
13. U. U., ii, 138. Cp. Lansac, op. cit., 41.
14. N. M., 14, 314, 450.
15. U. U., ii, 32.
16. Q. M., 46, 151, 285; U. U., i, S., 19, 20, 65; ii, 239, 241, 243, 265; iv, 192; N. M., 26, 375.
17. Compare this with Considerant's attempt to bring out this distinction in *Destinée Sociale*, vol. 1, 51. Quoted by Pinlocke, op. cit., 26.
18. Q. M., 118; N. M., 47.
19. N. M., 47. "They seek health, wealth and luxury."
20. U. U., iii, 339.
21. N. M., 69–70.
22. U. U., iii, 405–6.
23. U. U., iii, 406.
24. N. M., 77; this need for change and mania for variety is considered a vice in civilization, and yet it is a characteristic of many of the ways of nature, e.g. breeds need change, cross-fertilization, otherwise they degenerate; the soil gives of its best under a system of crop rotation; a varied diet gives pleasure and facilitates the digestion.
25. N. M., 72. Cp. "Une série passionée ne souffre pas des sectaires modérés; elle a horreur de la modération." U. U., iii, 405.
26. Q. M., 125.
27. N. M., 47; also U. U., ii, 239; iv, 11.
28. "L'inégalité est le ressort essentiel pour l'association, elle en est le moyen d'éxécution." N. M., 6; Cp. Q. M., 433, 436; N. M., 59.
29. N. M., 50.

30. Friendship is also a prevalent tendency from one to ten years, but it is at its height between ten to fifteen years.
31. See H. C. Barnard, *A History of English Education from 1760* (1961), 35, for this criticism of Rousseau.
32. U. U., iv, 2.
33. U. U., iv, 8.
34. Chapter on Little Hordes and Little Bands.
35. Chapter on sexual education; see also Manus. (1852), 188: "Pour le corps vigueur et dextérité pratique industrielle—Pour l'âme vertus naturelles, sciences théorique."
36. N. M., 55.
37. U. U., iii, 341.
38. N. M., 53.
39. N. M., 72.
40. U. U., iii, 407-8.
41. N. M., 77.
42. U. U., iii, 410.
43. "Le tableau de deux journées d'harmonies, un pauvre et un riche..." N. M., 67-8:

"*Journée de Lucas au mois de juin.*

Heures:
à 3½ lever, préparatifs,
à 4 séance à un groupe des écuries,
à 5 séance à un groupe de jardiniers,
à 7 le déjeuner,
à 7½ séance au groupe des faucheurs,
à 9½ séance au groupe de légumistes sous tente,
à 11 séance à la série des étables,
à 1 le diner,
à 2 séance à la série des silvains,
à 4 séance à un groupe de manufacture,
à 6 séance à la série d'arrosage,
à 8 séance à la bourse,
à 8½ le souper
à 9 séance fréquentation amusante,
à 10 le coucher.

Nota. On tient la bourse dans chaque phalange, non pas pour agioter sur la rente et les denrées, mais pour négocier les réunions de travail et de plaisir.

"J'ai supposé ici une journée à trois repas seulement, comme la seront celles des débutants en harmonie; mais quand elle sera en plein exercice, la vie active, l'habitude des séances courtes et variées donnera un prodigieux appétit: les etres nés et élevés dans l'harmonie seront obligés de faire cinq repas, et ce ne sera pas trop pour consommer l'immense quantité de vivres que produira ce nouvel ordre, où les riches varient leurs fonctions plus fréquemment que les pauvres ont plus d'appétit et de vigueur. C'est en tout point le contraire du mécanisme civilisé.

"Je vais décrire en cadre de cinq repas une journée d'homme riche,

THE PSYCHOLOGICAL BASIS

exerçant des fonctions plus variées que celles du précédent qui est un des villageois enrôlés au début.
"*Journée de Mondor en été*.
Heures. Sommeil de $10\frac{1}{2}$ du soir à 3 h. du matin.
à $3\frac{1}{2}$ lever, préparatifs,
à 4 cour du lever public, chronique de la nuit,
à $4\frac{1}{2}$ le délité, le repas suivi de la parade industrielle,
à $5\frac{1}{2}$ séance au groupe de la chasse,
à 7 séance au groupe de la pêche,
à 8 le déjeuner, les gazettes,
à 9 séance à un groupe de culture sous tente,
à 10 séance à la messe,
à $10\frac{1}{2}$ séance au groupe de la faisanderie,
à $11\frac{1}{2}$ séance à la bibliothèque,
à 1 Le Diner,
à $2\frac{1}{4}$ séance au groupe des serres fraîches,
à 4 séance au groupe des plantes exotiques,
à 5 séance au groupe des viviers,
à 6 le goûter à la campagne,
à $6\frac{1}{2}$ séance au groupe des mérinos,
à 8 séance à la bourse,
à 9 Le Souper, 5e repas,
à $9\frac{1}{2}$ séance cours des arts, concert, bal, spectacle, réceptions.
à $10\frac{1}{2}$ le coucher.
"On ne voit dans ce tableau que très peu d'instants laissés au sommeil: les harmoniens dormiront fort peu; l'hygiène raffinée, jointe à la variété des séances, les habitueront à ne pas se fatiguer dans les travaux; les corps ne s'useront pas dans la journée, n'auront besoin que d'un sommeil très court et s'y habitueront dès l'enfance, par une affluence de plaisirs auxquels la journée ne pourra pas suffire."

44. F. Zweig: *The Worker in an Affluent Society* (1961), 196–7.
45. U. U., iii, 341.
46. Fourier, like Plato and Rousseau before him, clearly recognized that "any reform of an existing order of things must be based on a reform in educational techniques and procedure". Mallinson, op. cit., 63.
47. N. M., 71.
48. Q. M., 417.
49. Manus. (1851), 23. "Je leur envie surtout la théorie des quatre passions cardinales par les sections coniques." [This was written in 1820.]
50. Fourier was familiar with Kepler's "Harmonices Mundi, ouvrage que Considerant me déclarait être une des sources des conceptions de Fourier." Lansac, op. cit., 54. Lansac was sometime private secretary to Considerant.
51. The similarity between his terminology and that used in present-day studies of similar problems is striking: both are derived from the vocabulary of geometry and analysis.
52. Quoted by Lansac, op. cit., 60.
53. Quoted by C. C. Granger, *La Mathématique Sociale du Marquis de Condorcet* (1956), 137.

54. Quoted by Lansac, op. cit., 60.
55. The mathematical study of abstract groups had its origin early in the nineteenth century.
56. For modern accounts of human groups see W. J. H. Sprott, *Science and Social Action* (1954), *Human Groups* (1958); C. M. Fleming, *Studies in the Social Psychology of Adolescence* (1951); J. Klein, *The Study of Groups* (1956); K. M. Evans, *Sociometry and Education* (1962).
57. Manus. (1851), 179.

CHAPTER THREE

The Aims of Education

A PEDAGOGICAL system, according to Durkheim, is born of the need to reflect on all the data of the educational situation instead of accepting them as unalterable facts; this need for reflection only arises intermittently when the times are out of joint and a co-ordinating principle is vital to restore order to society.[1] Fourier lived and wrote during such a period. The time of his early and formative years saw a most remarkable outburst of interest in education.[2] The dissemination of the ideas of the Enlightenment, the works of Rousseau, the demand for secular instruction, the recurrent crisis in recruitment within the Church, the suppression of the Society of Jesus creating as it did many vacancies in the colleges, were some of the causes which served to bring education to the forefront of public discussion.[3]

The social and philosophical theories of the Enlightenment were by the turn of the century widely known and their implications were much discussed.[4] The psychology of John Locke, introduced into France by Voltaire and systematized by Condillac, had been (to use Professor Barnard's phrase) out-Locked by Helvetius. Helvetius was able to assert that our species are indefinitely malleable: what makes one man different from another is his upbringing. "L'éducation nous fait ce que nous sommes"; consequently "L'éducation peut tout". D'Holbach likewise wrote: "L'instruction est le moyen le plus sûr d'inspirer aux peuples les sentiments, les talents, les idées, les vertus qui leur sont nécessaires."[5] This infinite faith in man's perfectability was perhaps most eloquently voiced and summarized by Condorcet. His optimism was widely shared. With the Revolution came the opportunity to actually change and reform the educational system. The difficulty and enormity of this task spelt inevitable defeat. Nevertheless during the years of the Convention (1792–95) all the educational questions that demanded attention and a solution in the nineteenth century were raised and debated.[6]

The aims of Fourier's educational proposals are threefold: (1) *political*, to improve the relationship between the different classes in society, (2) *psychological*, to make possible the unrestricted development and growth of individuals, and (3) *industrial* or *vocational*, to promote professional competence and satisfaction. These three subjects will be studied in turn in this chapter.

It is possible to find clear echoes of Fourier's educational aims and of his detailed proposals in the works of his predecessors and contemporaries. Yet, for all the detailed similarities of his educational aims with those of his predecessors, his emphasis is distinctive and the totality of his system remains different. His ideal society differs in essentials from any other formulated, and he is above all an original precursor in the attempt he makes to adapt education to the demands of industry. It is true that he states his case in the language of an extremist, but he insists that the various aspects of his proposals should be viewed as a whole. The success of his system of education "ne peut pas être jugé", he writes,[7] "sur des parcelles de théorie, c'est un vaste mécanisme, où chaque effet dérive des mouvements de l'ensemble, et des secours que se prêtent réciproquement les parties". It is necessary to see it as a whole before judging its merits or practicability.

Fourier is a great believer in the importance of education. "Il n'est pour l'homme aucun besoin plus urgent après la subsistance que l'éducation."[8] He sees in education a powerful and indispensable instrument of change to achieve his ideal society. Men and women, spoilt as they are by civilization, must be re-educated if they are to flourish in their new environment. "C'est donc par l'éducation qu'il faut commencer..."[9] Adults, Fourier admits, will find it difficult to adapt themselves to the new harmonious life; in the traditional stages, children under three years of age will be particularly precious, for unlike their elder brothers and sisters they would have remained unspoilt by civilized education.[10] Yet once harmonious society is established, education will still remain one of the most important branches of the social mechanism.[11] Education is of basic importance in his ideal society.

One purpose of Fourier's political organization is to establish social harmony; and education is one of his principal means of achieving this. In his own day he maintained there were three different types of education: academicians teaching the rich, masters teaching the middle class, and ushers teaching the poor. The consequence was that the rich were polished, the bourgeoisie mean, and the poor rough in their manners. The discord produced three different modes of behaviour and created rigid and harmful class divisions. His remedy is to give the same education to all classes.[12]

Contrast this with the attitude of his contemporary Fellenberg (1771–1844)[13] who had in 1799 made a similar criticism of the education of the day but had proposed radically different remedies. Fellenberg saw three types of education, one each for the upper, middle and lower classes. But far from wishing to abolish these differences, as Fourier desired, Fellenberg believed that it was important "to elevate those whose talents rendered them capable of it, to stations in which society could enjoy the utmost profit from their efforts; he believed that with the mass of the labouring classes, the only rational course was to prepare them for the station in which Providence had placed them, and to render them happy in it by raising them to their proper rank as rational and moral beings." The proper relation between the classes had to be maintained: the higher should appreciate and have sympathy for the lower; the lower should respect and love the higher. To accomplish this he would have them brought up side by side. Each could then observe and learn to value the other but without the necessity of mixing or associating. Fellenberg would educate all classes but give a separate and specially designed education to fit each individual to the class division to which God had seen fit to call him.[14]

Fourier does not believe that all men are equal, nor does he wish to make them so; but he does consider that an educational system can establish manners and attitudes that will make for pleasant and harmonious relationships in society. A shameful characteristic of civilization, says Fourier, is the coarseness and rudeness of the lower classes, and the difference between them and the higher classes in language and manners. This characteristic, says Fourier,[15] is believed necessary by many in civilization, as the labouring multitude, oppressed by poverty, would feel too keenly their misery if they were polished and educated. In Fourier's ideal state, however, it will no longer be necessary to brutalize the masses in order to inure them to hardship (for poverty will disappear), nor to fit them for the monotonous drudgery of labour (for all work will be attractive).

Attractive industry will render politeness and affability necessary among all classes. The meetings and intrigues of the groups of series can hardly be efficient or fruitful if the language and manners of both rich and poor are not identical and uniformly gracious. This general urbanity and unity of language and manners so necessary in Harmony, can only result from a uniform system of education. So education will be the principal means of reconciliation of rich and poor.[16] Harmonians will be drawn together by feelings of cordiality and friendship, unlike the civilized who detest each other. The phalange will come to consider itself a single united family, wherein it will not occur even to the most opulent to wish to deprive their children of an education which all others receive.[17]

The idea of education for all was being actively debated at the time Fourier wrote, and it was very variously interpreted. On the one hand, Diderot had held that all men from ministers down to the lowest peasants should be able to read, write and count; he did not believe, as did Rousseau, that knowledge and science might have a pernicious effect on labourers and peasants. "Loin de corrompre, l'instruction adoucit les caractères, éclaire sur les devoirs, subtilise les vices, les étouffe ou les voile."[18] The Physiocrats[19] had energetically demanded a free secular education for all, maintaining that education was a public service in a complete and integrated social organization, but within a framework of economic freedom.[20] Mirabeau was against a different education for rich and poor. He sees in education a means of creating loyalty to the government, and maintaining the stability of the State. He was perhaps the first man of his time to emphasize and advocate as an essential primary duty of the Sovereign the provision of education for all his people.[21]

On the other hand there is Rousseau. He is, as one would expect, contradictory: he is both cautious and extreme. He sees the need for further knowledge before a curriculum could be satisfactorily developed for the townsman. "Do not educate the town child for you do not know yet what suits him." As for the village child, "education does not suit him".[22] In *Emile* he writes, "The poor man has no need of an education, for his condition in life forces one upon him and he could receive no other."[23] Yet in his *Political Economy* Rousseau insists that education provided by the State should be common to all, and since, as he asserts, children mean more to the State than their parents, they should not be abandoned to their parents' educational whims and fancies. "If children are brought up together in the bosom of equality", he says, "if they are penetrated with the laws of the state and with the principle of the general will, if they are educated to respect them above all else . . . let us not doubt that they will also cherish each other with the mutual affection of brothers, wish only for what society wants and instead of the vain gossip of citizens will substitute the activity of men and citizens and become one day the defenders and fathers of their country, whose children they have been so long."[24]

La Chalotais, though he believed in the perfectibility of man through education, was forthright in his condemnation of education of the masses. "Le bien de la société demande que les connaissances du peuple ne s'extendent pas plus loin que ses occupations."[25] "The last thing he desired", writes Fontainerie, "was any increase in educational opportunity for the people in general."[26]

It is true that the Constitution of 1793 had promised "une instruction commune" (Article 122) and had asserted that education was everyone's business. "La société doit favoriser de tout son pouvoir les progrès de la raison publique et mettre l'instruction à la portée de tous les citoyens." (Article 22).[27] But these were vague aspirations which had yet to be developed, clarified, and implemented. Thus, coupled with the already divergent views as to who should receive instruction, there also developed a sharp division of opinion as to what, how and where they should be taught. The proceedings of the various education committees and the numerous pamphlets of the time bear witness to the immense and frequently fundamental divergence of views. The proposals of Condorcet, to provide in five stages[28] a free, compulsory and secular education were not finally effectively implemented until the 1959 education re-organization in France.[29] Among the various alternatives to the Condorcet project was the Lepeletier plan propagated by the Montagnards, which has particularly striking similarities with Fourier's proposals.[30]

The Lepeletier plan was presented to the National Convention by Maximilien Robespierre in 1793, soon after its author had been assassinated,[31] and both in view of the circumstances and the extremity of its proposals received wide publicity and aroused a storm of discussion; but opinion was generally hostile to it and it was withdrawn. Lepeletier claims that the purpose of education is "former les hommes, propager les connaissances humaines". These are two sides of the problem that must be resolved: "La première constitue l'éducation, la seconde l'instruction."[32]

The intention of Lepeletier was to develop further at the primary stage Condorcet's plan which he found "very satisfactory". The higher grades of education as conceived by Condorcet catered for the instruction of an elite and these in themselves were satisfactory. But Lepeletier claimed that Condorcet's plans neglected the education of the people. Lepeletier sets out to create a system of education that would suit all and would represent the debt of the nation to all: "en un mot, une éducation vraiment et universellement nationale".[33] Lequinio takes up a similar attitude: "A common education", he says, "is the only perfectly republican one; it is the only one capable of destroying the foolish pride which torments the human race and which private education will always nourish even when fathers and teachers make a point of destroying it early; it is the only education which will excite emulation without feeding vanity, it is the only one which will form man to the love of work, to the habit of sobriety, to the scorn of a luxurious or voluptuous existence and to the necessity of seeing his happiness inseparable from that of the public happiness; it is the only one in a word which will bring about the realization of the motherland."[34]

Lepeletier's method is to create a communal education for all: boys 5–12 years, girls 5–11 years. The plan was to set up residential schools where all would receive the same food, clothing, instruction and care.[35] The larger part of the day would be spent in manual labour.[36] Here again although there are striking similarities with Fourier's schemes, fundamental differences are conspicuous. Michel Lepeletier's attitude was inspired to some extent by an admiration for Sparta:[37] he wished to train children to do without the luxuries and many of the necessities of life.[38] This from a kind of puritan zeal, whereas Fourier was on the contrary not simply hedonistic but wished to use normal manual training to prepare children for professional life. For Fourier manual labour is not only an exercise or a recreation but vocational training and indeed life itself.

Condorcet was obsessed with equality. "L'inégalité d'instruction est une des principales sources de la tyrannie."[39] He believed that the establishment of equality among nations and man would mean the attainment of the real perfection of man. The extension of education for all would bring with it happiness, improved morals, good government and the disappearance of boredom for mankind[40] but it was essential that instruction should be given "en commun, et les femmes ne doivent pas être exclues de l'enseignement".[41] The revolutionaries—notably the Plaine, Montagne, Gironde[42]—were, in the main, in general agreement with these sentiments, but they differed as to the reasons and methods of attaining them. The members of the Plaine for example—since they were principally concerned with liberty—respected the rights of parents and were prepared to tolerate private and Catholic schools alongside the state system. Others, overwhelmingly preoccupied with equality, emphasized the need for a state monopoly of education and the creation of secular comprehensive schools (l'école unique) for all children in the district.[43] This they believed, as did Lepeletier, was the only way to abolish class differences and create satisfactory citizens for the Republic.

Fourier's proposals were that education should be communal, residential, free, universal but not compulsory. The intrinsic superiority of his methods will, he claims, attract rich and poor alike, and compulsion will prove superfluous.[44] His system will provide for all a common education irrespective of prospective careers or present or future wealth.

The education of the individual, says Fourier, must be based on his needs and these needs arise from the nature of man. Spontaneity and freedom are essential, but perhaps paradoxically Fourier maintains that man's needs and desires require development, training and education. "L'homme ne reçoit de la nature que des germes, que l'éducation doit développer. L'éducation est pour l'homme une seconde mère; sans elle il se trouve ravalé fort au-dessous de la nature."[45] Rousseau too had expressed a somewhat similar view when he had written in his *Emile*: "All that we have not at our birth but which we need when we are grown is given us by education."[46] Education for Fourier meant the full development of man's potentialities expressed and guided solely by attraction. Man can never be satisfied, at peace with himself, with his fellows and with God, as long as he remains hindered and thwarted in his endeavours at self-expression.[47] Education must concern itself fully with all aspects of body and mind,[48] developing these harmoniously and aiming at perfection in all respects.[49]

The problem, says Fourier, is to enable all children to develop vigorous minds and bodies, and acquire industrial dexterity and knowledge; this aim must be achieved without any recourse to parental or school authority and only while allowing each child "la plus absolue liberté".[50] This absolute freedom, so indispensable for full individual growth and development, can only be found, argues Fourier, within the collectively organized series and groups. Education must therefore be collective if the child is to acquire "une vigeur et une dexterité prodigieuse inconnues aujourd'hui".[51] The failure of civilized education to produce fully developed all-rounded men is, in the main, because collective education is impossible in civilization.[52]

The individual's psychological and physiological needs must be fully satisfied but these Fourier is aware can only be satisfied within society. Fourier perceived, as do modern educationalists,[53] that education can only be within a society and that there can be no society without education. His educational proposals, he claims, are so designed as to train the child in the absolute maximum individual utilization of freedom, and at the same time, while in no way restricting individual desire, directing his energies to increasing the social well-being of the whole community.[54] Fourier believes that it is the task of harmonious education to enable the child freely and spontaneously, on his own accord, to seek, demand and carry out this training. Fourier's aims may seem to be contradictory and incompatible, in the sense that he wants his pupils to be entirely free and at the same time useful servants of society. However, the precise purpose of his ideal state is to end this tradition of antagonism. He tries to confine in one unified scheme ideas which had been formerly proposed or considered only in isolated parts.

Education must help man to attain perfect utilization of all instincts, talents and drives God has given him. It is erroneous, Fourier argues, to instil the principles of virtue and duty into a child at an early age (or for that matter at any time); and expect him to guide his actions along the lines laid down by morality. This will only lead to abysmal failure: it is contrary to the nature of a child. In enforcing an *a priori* pattern of behaviour upon the child, the scope for free and spontaneous development is limited. Moreover, Fourier believes that opinions on the upbringing of children are arbitrary and contradictory, for example, "un moraliste opinéra pour élèver l'enfant au mépris des richesses perfides et à l'amour de la vérité; un économiste voudra qu'on l'élève à l'amour du trafic et du mensonge—deux choses inséparables".[55] Virtue, the love of the good and the beautiful, important though they may be, are among the last results of an education. The first task of education must be the development of the "dexterity and health of the child".[56]

Secondly, once the body has been prepared as it were, the development of the child's mental capacities, his intellectual and spiritual resources, can proceed. Thus Fourier, like Rousseau, emphasizes the physical aspect of education (the development of the senses and increase in muscular ability) in infancy and childhood; and only later in adolescence and early manhood does he allow the mental aspects preponderance.[57] The central aim throughout, however, is the "unitary cultivation of the twelve passions".[58]

Fourier emphasizes the extreme importance of early childhood[59] and his aim is to lay the foundations of all subsequent growth and development in the first few years. From the beginning good physical health is fostered through the provision of adequate accommodation, physical exercise, wholesome food and medical care.[60] The child is encouraged to take a pride in his own developed abilities and respect those of others. The organization of natural education in "series"[61] will, argues

Fourier, create the necessary conditions for spontaneous and unrestricted activity for each child, which is at the same time not offensive or harmful to other children and members of the phalange. This aim, coupled as it is with the inculcation of the social graces (explained above) and the development of vocational desires (see below), is to establish in each child sufficient enthusiasm, curiosity and confidence to utilize its energy to capacity in the varied pursuits of the phalange. The foundations will have been laid by $4\frac{1}{2}$–5 years[62] but as the individual grows so his opportunities will increase. As his practical knowledge of life widens, so he will come to realize the need for a theoretical understanding of the principles involved. He will see the need for academic study and will himself seek instruction and enlightenment[63] by presenting himself to a chosen teacher at the school or academy.

The aim for the individual must be the prevention of frustration through unrestricted opportunity for self-expression. Civilized education, says Fourier, can see nothing but vice in all the impulses that nature has given the child.[64] It therefore attempts to change our natural instincts. The freedom of the child is removed; and the consequent inability of the child to satisfy his natural desires creates his anti-social behaviour. This repression creates great unhappiness for child and parent. It is inevitable, says Fourier, that in civilization the restriction of freedom of expression should lead in childhood to what is considered bad and vicious consequences.[65] Children become lazy and diabolical, destructive and greedy, quarrelsome and insolent.

It shows, Fourier thinks, a lack of understanding of the laws of God to criticize the behaviour of children in civilized society. It is, for example, the generally held view among fathers and teachers that children are lazy; yet nothing is further from the truth. Children of 2 or 3 years are extremely industrious;[66] that they later become lazy is a mere consequence of inappropriate educational methods. The civilized cannot make use of the freedom of self-expression for they lack the necessary understanding of the laws of nature to create an appropriate organization, viz. Harmonious Association, which will reconcile the freedom of the individual and of society. The organization of civilized society is wrong and the methods employed in educational practice therein only serve to create those very vices the civilized so abhor. In associative education, the aim is to use these very same instincts or impulses, which produce vices in civilization, in such a way as to yield unprecedented individual pleasure and increased wealth for the whole community.

The discovery of the aptitudes and the abilities of all children and the creation of a love for productive labour is a primary and fundamental task of Harmonious education.[66] Others before him had, of course, advocated the need to develop manual skills and create a love for labour. The educational practices of the early monks, based on the teaching of the rabbis of pre-Christian days and the example of the Carpenter of Nazareth, laid great stress upon manual labour.[67] The development of the idea of a wider concept of instruction and education, more practical and less academic, more concrete and less abstract, increasingly based on the child's immediate environment and his personal inexperience rather than on *a priori* concepts, is of course a main theme of the history of educational ideas. Durkheim has shown how, although many of its beginnings can be traced to earlier times, the French Revolution inaugurated what he calls the Age of Realism (l'age réaliste) in pedagogical practice. The trend was towards modern subjects with a scientific, utilitarian and nationalistic bias. The new pedagogy was radically opposed to the old: its chief concern now was with the material world and not with abstract human values; it was now realistic whereas before it had been humanistic.[68]

The need to widen the curriculum, to broaden the field of study, and to link it with everyday things had been discussed by many of the early thinkers. The precursors of the Age of Realism were many and notable. Bacon and Comenius, for example, were early critics of a purely formal curriculum. Luther in his writing had stressed the need for linking industry and school.[69] Children were to spend one or two hours daily at school, the remainder of the time was principally to be occupied learning a trade in their own home.[70] Rabelais saw the advantages of approaching the abstract through the concrete and the personal. He believed in teaching boys to play musical instruments, ride, swim, handle boats and excel in military warfare. He seems to accept the attitude of the Greek citizen to manual labour, though he sees advantage in it as a means of recreation.

Knowledge of handicrafts and industry is to be gained through observation only.[71] Mulcaster, by including singing, playing a musical instrument and drawing, definitely widened the school curriculum of his time, but he was really interested in the gifted few.[72]

Although John Locke was primarily concerned with the education of an English Gentleman, his work had considerable influence on the whole range of education and far beyond his native land. Locke wished his young pupil to learn one manual trade, and possibly for the more energetic, one or two others, chosen from a wide variety.[73] The acquisition of these manual skills were not intended by Locke to be taken too seriously. Their aim was to exercise the body, and provide diversion and relaxation for the mind. For the poor, Locke suggested the establishment of workhouse schools, for children aged 3 to 14 years. Here the aim was the formation of orderly habits, discipline and sobriety.[74]

"I insist absolutely", wrote Rousseau, "that Emile shall learn a trade . . ."[75] Rousseau's educational ideas crop up in the various educational projects of the period; but it is outside France, particularly in the Protestant countries, that his influence was most felt and gave rise to pedagogic experimentation.[76] Pestalozzi was the first great educator to apply the principles of Rousseau. Pestalozzi demonstrated that manual and physical work and intellectual activity could go together. Froebel, who was to demonstrate the creative value of practical activity in infant education, was almost certainly unknown to Fourier. Fourier had read about the work of Pestalozzi in the newspapers, but dismisses his views in a couple of sentences.[77] Fourier hardly ever refers to his predecessors or contemporaries, and when he does so it is very briefly and inadequately. Some similarities do exist between him and Pestalozzi: these are discussed later.

Professor Dobinson has clearly traced the historical origins and shown how after a lapse of about 150 years attempts are now being made to establish the Revolutionary concept of the worker citizen.[78] "This was of a worker", Professor Dobinson writes, "trained as an efficient producer, as a citizen aware of his rights and responsibilities, and as a man appreciating the best in culture. It is an ideal difficult to attain but none the worse for that."[79] This concept was slow in finding support. Its meaning and implication had to be developed and understood. Fourier's originality lies in that he stressed the importance of the individual in industry as a human being with desires and needs, and he clearly foresaw the necessity to work out in detail the educational implications. In his emphasis on the infinite connections between education and society he goes far beyond the demands made by his predecessors or contemporaries for a closer relationship between school and workshop. He includes all aspects of social life and not merely manual and industrial activity, as points of contact between school and society. Fourier believes "that work can be transformed and turned into a joy, triumphing over its weariness and its pain". Fourier saw, as did A. N. Whitehead much later, that this was the "sole real hope of toiling humanity".[80] Fourier did not believe that "the curse that had been laid upon humanity, in fable and in fact, [was] that by the sweat of its brow shall it live".[81] Fourier, like the mad priest in Bernard Shaw's *John Bull's Other Island*, dreamed of "a commonwealth in which work is play and play is life . . ."[82] The problem, as Fourier saw it, was to analyse each individual's vocations and then develop them fully. He is original in showing that education is a continuous integral, and not a part-time, process. He shows that education involves integrated development of all faculties and that it is necessary to approach them through tendencies—physical, moral, or intellectual—which may predominate at any given stage of development; and all this to take place within the child's own surroundings. The whole of his education system is directed towards achieving these ends.

The problem of vocational guidance ("la question de la vocation ou instinct de fonctions sociales"[83]) is, says Fourier, a fundamental aspect of education, and yet in civilization it remains unknown (or obscure).[84] It is true that Rousseau had emphasized the need to know the child and to discover his bent before embarking upon his education,[85] but he does not develop this point. Nor does there seem to be any detailed discussion on the problem of the discovery of abilities, when Fourier was writing, since the time of Plato. The work of the Spanish doctor Juan Huarte (1562–89) is an exception; but Huarte seems to have interested himself mainly in discovering methods which would "tell whether anyone wishing to study dialectics, philosophy, medicine, theology or law had the genius required to study any of these sciences".[86] Fourier, however, is concerned with the whole community—rich and poor alike—and he does not confine his efforts to selecting and training academics, top executives or rulers. His aim is to see that each individual's potentialities—manual, sensual, intellectual—are discovered, and that they then all find pleasure and satisfaction in industrial productivity.[87] He is perhaps the first to *seek* to develop an experimentally based child guidance psychology integrated within an educational system.

At least nine-tenths of the civilized community, Fourier claims, would readily change their jobs, or are in jobs they have been forced into by parental pressure or economic necessity. This, he says, can but lead to frustration, boredom and unhappiness. The situation, of course, will be different in the phalange, for there education never develops a single vocation in the child, but thirty graduated vocations, with varying degrees of dominance.[88] This wide vocational training will enable each individual to practise many different and unrelated crafts. Rich and poor alike will participate in a great variety of jobs, and so, in addition to earning a secure living, will widen their horizons and increase their interests and opportunities. Indeed, in association, the very nature and purpose of work is different—industrial affluence, important though it is, is never an end in itself. Work is rather an indispensable means for man's fulfilment. Fourier does not measure work solely in terms of the profitability of the capital invested. His is a multidimensional scale: Capital, Talent, Labour, receive a fixed proportion of the profit and the return must be satisfactory to each partner. Individual and social factors are thus not ignored —unpleasant or abhorrent work will not be sufficiently attractive and will therefore not be undertaken.

It is the task of harmonious education to reconcile man and industrial labour. The problem is, believes Fourier, basically no different from the cultivation of a feeling and desire for good food or music. Pleasure and appreciation of good cooking require experience and much study, likewise industrial skill needs to be learned before it can yield satisfaction (in a different way but on the same level).

THE AIMS OF EDUCATION 45

The divorce between life and labour can be prevented by the early introduction of children into the market-gardens, fields, workshops and kitchens of the phalange.[89] There they will observe their elders (as well as other children slightly older than themselves), and the wish to emulate them will be born. Opportunities for so doing will be provided in miniature workshops suitable for these children and also for those with more developed skills, who will all be given every encouragement to help the adults in real life production. The principle laid down by Fourier, for all training in agrarian and technical pursuits, is first to acquire the skill practically on the spot, in the actual workshop or in the field; and, only secondly, if the child is sufficiently interested and so desires, are the theoretical aspects to be pursued. It is necessary to educate practical farmers, market-gardeners, manufacturers, before attempting to give a theoretical or academic exposition and training.[90] Academic, bookish education, unrelated to practice, is no introduction to industrial work. The vast majority of children are bored and repelled by it[91].

These are all contemporary problems and it is interesting to note that solutions very similar to those advocated by Charles Fourier are being found. In our own country, sandwich and full-time technological courses are increasing in popularity, but the opportunities for industrial training remain limited. Indeed our economic situation makes it imperative that we consider more carefully whether we ought not to provide facilities for "industrial training as part of a general educational process in which every young person with ability and interest has the right to take part".[92] In Russia, a two-year stint in productive labour was compulsory for all except the very best before admission to higher education. In China, children at a very early age are shown round the farms and factories, while older children and students, for a few hours a week, work and receive tuition in the factories and communes[93].

But in this area of educational endeavour much remains to be learnt. For as Professor Lauwerys has written "All this may be valuable; but how far it succeeds in really making people appreciate the value of hard and tiring work is questionable. Schools have been urged to make products which can be sold; but such measures—as the experience of India has shown—are unlikely to be fruitful. Nevertheless, efforts will surely be continued."[94]

1. Cp. article on Pédagogie in Buisson, *Nouveau dictionnaire de pédagogie et d'instruction primaire* (1911), 1841 (b).
2. See e.g. René Hubert, *Histoire de la Pédagogie* (1949); Maurice Gontard, *L'Enseignement Primaire en France (1789–1833)* (1959), 52.
3. Cp. James Guillaume's Introduction to *Procès-verbaux du Comité d'instruction publique*. Ass. Legis., p. x, etc.
4. D. Mornet: *Les origines intellectuelles de la Révolution* (1933), 420.
5. Quoted by Gontard, op. cit., 58.
6. Hubert, *Histoire*, op. cit., 74.
7. U. U., iv, 38.
8. Cp. with Danton's statement: "après le pain, l'éducation est le premier besoin des peuples", quoted by Gontard, op. cit., 99.
9. N. M., 167.
10. Q. M., 308.
11. U. U., iv, 209.
12. U. U., iv, 4, 5. See also U. U., i, S., 157.
13. C. A. Bennett: *History of Manual and Industrial Education up to 1870* (Illinois, 1929), 128, 129.
14. Ibid., 129.
15. U. U., iv, 4.
16. See also U. U., iv, 383.
17. U. U., iv, 6.
18. Quoted by Gontard, op. cit., 58.
19. See Gontard, op. cit., 59.
20. Cp. Gourdon: "Les physiocrates et l'éducation au XVIIIe siècle" in *Revue Pédagogique* (1901), I, 577–89.
21. Gontard, op. cit., 60.
22. *Nouvelle Héloïse* (1761), vii, 290.
23. Payne's ed., 20.
24. *Econ. politique*, 4, 423–424; quoted by M. H. Johnes, *Influence of the Philosophy of Progress on French Educational Theory and Practice from 1789–1848*, Ph. D. Wales, 1952, 61–2.
25. La Chalotais, *Essai d'éducation nationale* (1763), 26.
26. F. de la Fontainerie, *French liberalism and education in the Eighteenth Century* (1932), see Introduction, 35.
27. Quoted by Gontard, op. cit., 104.
28. "Les écoles primaires, les écoles secondaires (écoles primaires supérieures), les Instituts (collèges), les lycées (facultés), et la Société des Sciences et des Arts, chargée de la Direction génerale de l'Enseignement." J. Palmero, *Histoire des Institutions et des Doctrines Pédagogiques par les textes* (1952), 251.
29. For a comparison in tabular form of the proposals of Condorcet and the actual situation in 1960 see *Encyclopédie Pratique de l'Education en France* (1960), 18.

THE AIMS OF EDUCATION 47

30. Other plans were for example those proposed by Daunou, Lakanal, and Sièyes (see Gontard, op. cit., 107). They are not considered here since they have nothing in common with Fourier's ideas.
31. Michel Lepeletier (1760–1793), ex-Marquis de Saint-Fargeau, member of States-General (1789) and president of the National Assembly (1790); member of the National Convention (1792); a Montagnard deputy who was assassinated on 20 January 1793.
32. J. Guillaume, *Procès-Verbaux du Comité d'instruction publique*, Convention Nationale, 2, 35.
33. Ibid., 36.
34. J. M. Lequinio, *Discours sur l'éducation commune* (1793), 2–3, quoted by Johnes, op. cit., 146.
35. J. Guillaume, op. cit., 55.
36. Ibid., 57.
37. See Gontard, op. cit., 107; St. Just, Lepeletier and the Montagnards however, also owe some of their inspiration to the work of Malby and Morelly (see supra).
38. J. Guillaume, op. cit., 50. Cp. "Les enfants seront couchés durement, leur nourriture sera saine, mais frugale, leur vêtement commode, mais grossier." No distinction (between rich and poor) will be made. 42.
39. *Oeuvres*, vii, 171.
40. Cp. Gontard, op. cit., 88–9.
41. *Oeuvres*, vii, 220.
42. Gontard, op. cit., 99.
43. Gontard, op. cit., 99.
44. U. U., iv, 52.
45. U. U., iv, 274.
46. *Emile*, Payne's ed., 2.
47. U. U., iii, 239.
48. U. U., iv, 7.
49. U. U., iv, 2, 299. "Introduisant la perfection sur tous les points." (2) "Elevant à la perfection tous les ressorts corporels et spirituels." (299)
50. Manus. (1851), 113; cp. Manus. (1852), 298.
51. Q. M., 95, 96.
52. U. U., iv, 30.
53. See for example René Hubert, *Traité de pédagogie générale* (1946), 38.
54. Manus. (1852), 186.
55. U. U., iv, 11.
56. U. U., iv, 11.
57. U. U., iv, 71, 75, 115, 116.
58. Où veut (l'attraction) nous conduire: 1. Au luxe 2. Auxgroupes. 3. Aux séries. A l'UNITE. C'est sur ces impulsions générales que doit se guider la politique de l'éducation." U. U., iv, 11.
59. Q. M., 308, U. U., iv, 27.
60. U. U., iv, 66; for details and methods he advocates see Chapter 5.
61. Q. M., 96, also U. U., iv, 54.
62. U. U., iv, 12.
63. N. M., 295.

64. U. U., iv, 158, 299–300.
65. U. U., iv, 41, 94, 274; N. M., 180, 186, 412.
66. N. M., 181.
66. U. U., iv, 3; N. M., 167.
67. W. P. Sears, *The Roots of Vocational Education* (1931), 77; C. H. Dobinson, *Year Book of Education*, 1958: The French "Centres d'Apprentissage".
68. E. Durkheim, *L'Evolution Pédagogique en France* (1938), 2, 151–2.
69. Sears, op. cit., 83.
70. A. Léon, *Histoire de l'Education Technique* (1961), 27.
71. Bennett, op. cit., 33.
72. Ibid., 33.
73. For a critical study and assessment of the educational ideas of John Locke, see V. Mallinson in *Les Grands Pédagogues* (1961), 125–43.
74. A. Léon, op. cit., 31; see also M. G. Mason, "John Locke's Proposals on Work-House Schools", *Durham Research Review*, Sept. 1962, 8–16.
75. *Emile*, Payne's edition, 180. But he goes on: "I do not want him to be an embroiderer, a gilder, or a varnisher, like Locke's gentlemen . . ." Rousseau prefers him to be a carpenter so that he might be in a position to earn his living should there occur a political upheaval.
76. Léon, op. cit., 35.
77. N. M., 240.
78. *Year Book of Education* (1958), the French *"Centre d'Apprentissage"*, 186.
79. He believes that "there is even today no better formulation than that written by Condorcet in 1793: 'We shall prove that, by a suitable choice of syllabus and of methods of education, we can teach the citizen everything that he needs to know in order to be able to manage his household, administer his affairs and employ his labour and his faculties in freedom; to know his rights and to be able to exercise them; to be acquainted with his duties and fulfil them satisfactorily; to judge his own and other men's actions according to his own lights and to be a stranger to none of the high and delicate feelings which honour human nature . . .' " See *Progress of the Human Mind*, 182.
80. A. N. Whitehead, *The Aims of Education* (1951), 67–8.
81. Ibid., 67.
82. Quoted by Whitehead, 66.
83. U. U., iv, 3.
84. "Il n'est donc pas de question plus obscure parmi nous que celle . . ." U. U., iv, 3.
85. See e.g. *Emile*, Payne's ed., 60, 61.
86. Quoted in *Year Book of Education*, 1955, 75.
87. N. M., 167.
88. U. U., iv, 3.
89. N. M., 294.
90. N. M., 294.
91. N. M., 295; Cp. Professor Dobinson on "excessive bookishness of grammar school pupils" and "provision for manual skills" in his *Technical Education for Adolescents* (1951), 77, 101.
92. See the article "Industrial Training for all, Mirage or Reality?" in

The Times Educational Supplement, 27 March 1964, 794; Cp. Gertrude Williams, *Apprenticeship in Europe. The Lesson for Britain* (1963).

93. See N. S. Khrushchev's Memorandum on "Strengthening the ties of the School with Life", September 1958; also, for example, F. Greene, *The Wall has Two Sides* (1962).

94. J. A. Lauwerys, "China", in E. J. King, *Communist Education* (1963), 279.

CHAPTER FOUR

Parents and Teachers: the Organization of Teaching

FOURIER believes that education ought to be communal. The home, asserts Fourier, is unsuitable for educating young children. The child must be brought up as a member of the larger social unit of the phalange. Unlike Rousseau and Pestalozzi, he has no use for family education. He discerns little but evil in the influence of the family and its servants on the growing child. Like Plato he wants to destroy the family as a social and educational unit.[1]

Fourier is against marriage because he considers it has harmful effects upon society. Marriage, he maintains, binds two people in a league against all that surrounds them and makes them indifferent to public misfortunes; the highest praise that can be given to anyone is to say that marriage has not changed him.[2] Marriage thus prevents man from entering into wider social relations, extending his horizons and undertaking new and perhaps hazardous tasks.

Fourier's championship of the feminist cause also led him to advocate an end to marriage and family life. "There has never been a more zealous, if perhaps injudicious defender of women than Fourier. No one has emphasized more strongly that in civilization woman is 'made for slavery' and that given a chance, she is fit for better things."[3] Woman, once liberated from her domestic servitude and constant surveillance of her children and instead given the opportunity to compete with the male in all occupations, will acquire the dignity, personality and privileges now only available to men. This economic and professional liberation, this new found independence for women, says Fourier, will lead to a revolution in social and sexual morals.[4] A new and true freedom will prevail—for

God recognizes as a freedom only that which is extended to both sexes and not to one alone.[5]

But Fourier is against the family on educational grounds as well. Rousseau had advocated in his *Emile* that "the child's natural teachers are his parents, and there is no real education outside the family".[6] This, says Fourier, can only lead to irreparable harm. The father will desire to bring up his child in his own mould and yet the talents and abilities of his son may be totally different.[7] The father will attempt to instil his own ideals of success into his child and these will usually be unsuitable for the aptitudes and temperament of the offspring. Moreover, asserts Fourier, family education puts the father in a false position for he is not his son's natural disciplinarian.[8]

"The right nurse is the mother", Rousseau proclaims,[9] but Fourier had apparently seen too many mothers who were unable to cope with their offspring and he does not agree. The mother may be delicate, or in ill health, or may be interested in other pursuits; consequently others better qualified and by nature more suitable ought to take over.[10]

The home, asserts Fourier, is unsuitable on a further count: the resources available to parents are limited; this restricts the provision of educational material. Moreover, when brought up within the family circle, the growing child is subject to the conflict and distrust between the parents, the school, his peers and the servants.[11] At school, says Fourier, he may be taught to 'spurn perfidious riches' or to admire the virtues of the young republicans of Sparta and 'similar nonsense'. It is true, continues Fourier, that among all this there are some excellent precepts, but the child in the family milieu absorbs only the most dangerous anti-social tenets and spurns the little good there is. The family influence is too strong for it to be otherwise. The father, acting always in secret, will early impress upon his child the need to outwit others, by means foul or fair, where monetary considerations are involved. The child will thus early appreciate that money made at the expense of someone else is a true sign of ability and of success. True, he adds, possibly one eighth or more likely one sixteenth of parents are exempt from this radical vice in family education, but they are exceptions.

Other conflicts too, says Fourier, give rise to difficulties. Children, particularly of rich parents, have rigorous rules laid down for their behaviour. The wish of parents to bring them up unspoilt inevitably makes them unreasonable. The child, in assocation with his peers, because of the restrictions of his freedom, develops the desire to oppose on all points, and this opposition is further strengthened by the gang (cabalistic) spirit. The valets, moreover, usually relax the rules and allow concessions, which then necessitate a secret conspiracy between servant and child to keep the parents in ignorance. This private arrangement gives the valet some power over his charge, sometimes to the detriment of both. Similar quarrels may also arise between father and mothers.

Later, on the threshold of the adult world, a young person will be the subject of an altogether different education.[12] He will now be taught to discard the morality of the classroom as fit only for schooldays and urged to adopt an adult attitude. He will learn to indulge in pleasures regardless of what he had previously been taught. He will learn of the pleasures associated with the love of money and ambition, and will "communiquer sa dépravation à toutes les fillettes qu'il peut fréquenter".[13] These various conflicting views, Fourier concludes, give rise to emotional insecurity and a need for the child to display contradictory attitudes in differing situations.

Fourier desires to eradicate these difficulties and his solution is simply the abolition of the family. Plato had suggested that wife and children should be in common; and that no parent should know his own child nor any child his parent.[14] Although Aristotle argued that this notion of a community of wives and children would be attended with many difficulties[15] it remained a current theme in the plans of successive reformers, notably Campanella and Enfantin. In the early years of the Soviet Union libertarian attitudes towards marriages were encouraged for a time, and family ties were weakened as far as possible, but in the 1930s this policy was reversed.[16] "More recently . . . the socialists, who at one time were singing paeons in favour of free love, have taken up a more conciliatory attitude towards marriage, chiefly insisting on easier divorce."[17]

A solution, less radical but not dissimilar to that advocated by Fourier, has been found by the pioneer communal settlers of Israel. In the "classical" Kibbutz, the child is removed from the parents at birth and brought up by the community.[18] He rarely sees his parents for more than a few hours a day. This is precisely, as we shall see in detail, what Fourier sought for his phalange, and the advantages the settlers give are not dissimilar to Fourier's. "The two things stressed", writes Dr. John Bowlby, "were, first, emancipation of women from both domestic chores and economic dependence on husbands, and, second, benefit to the children. Such benefit, it is held, is of two kinds. On the one hand, it is preferable for babies and children to be brought up by trained nurses: both their physical and mental health will benefit if they are preserved from the ignorance, inexperience and possibly pathogenic emotions of parents. On the other hand, it is never too young to become attuned to group living and to learn to co-operate and to share."[19]

In Fourier's system, children are brought up by the community and their home is the phalange. Special trained nurses, the bonnins, look after the children until they are four and a half, but from then the responsibility for the child's progress, education and training becomes one for all within the phalange willing and able to bestow it. As soon as they can, children are free to participate in any group or activity of the community, and it is there that they will receive help, encouragement and instruction from those better endowed or more experienced. The children will thus grow up learning to fend for themselves, and learning from those around them.

Fourier believes that the child's best and natural teacher is one slightly older, and not the parent or teacher. His plans for the education and training of children are firmly based upon this principle—"*le mutualisme composé convergent, bien différent du mutualisme simple récemment introduit dans les écoles civilisées*".[20] Fourier, that is, proposed an adaptation of the Bell and Lancaster method.[21] At the time when he was writing, this method was finding much favour in France. It culminated in the formation of "la Société pour l'instruction élémentaire" in 1815, and branches were opened in the provinces, at Arras, Bordeaux, Poitiers, Nantes, Lyon and in Fourier's native Besançon. In November 1818, there were forty-two of them.[22]

The monitorial system, although not new, was, particularly between 1815 and 1820, in the forefront of French educational controversy. In newspaper articles, pamphlets, and booklets, the merits of the system propounded by Dr. Bell (1753–1832) and

Joseph Lancaster (1778–1838) were explained, analysed and discussed.[23]

The system consisted in setting children to teach children, and it was now being developed to educate children on a large and organized scale. The use of monitors enabled the teacher to keep all the children occupied, and eliminated the time previously wasted by the pupils while one of their number was receiving instruction. The monitors in Lancaster's school had extraneous duties. "When a child was admitted, a monitor assigned him to his class; while he remained a monitor taught him (with nine other pupils); when he was absent one monitor ascertained the fact, and another found the reason; a monitor examined him periodically, and when he made progress a monitor promoted him; a monitor ruled the writing paper, a monitor made or mended the pens; a monitor had charge of the slates and books; and a monitor-general looked after all the other monitors."[24] The adult in charge, who was now left to concentrate mainly on the organization and discipline of the school, could control a much larger number of children.

But for some of the advocates of the system in France in 1815, the usual method was much more than a mere pedagogic procedure. They argued that the main benefit would be derived by the children themselves. The 'instituteurs' may well be more knowledgeable but it was preferable that children instruct themselves. His self-esteem and reputation at stake, a child is more likely to give better instruction. Moreover, he is the more likely to understand the difficulties, and would find it easier to get on with his contemporaries. The monitor's authority, based merely on superior learning and merit, will be willingly acknowledged by his inferiors, who, so the argument continues, will willingly follow his lead. But the self-esteem and pride of the inferior will encourage the less endowed to greater efforts, so that they may in their turn become monitors.

> "Athlètes sémillants dont la rivalité
> S'accord avec les jeux, les sauts et la gaîté."[25]

This system of rewards, with fierce competiton for places, with some pushing for promotion, while others try hard not to yield, will create in the class, it was hoped, a salutary improvement in study.

The system will, others also argued, give a training in political and social duties and responsibilities of the citizen. In the traditional establishments, the child threatened with sanctions automatically obeyed the teacher. Under the monitorial system, some hoped that the child would learn more about his obligations and duties, and the need to obey. Some went so far as to advocate the allocation of punishment by a children's jury. Children punished by a jury of their peers, it was argued, were less likely to acquire the habit of lying and more likely to receive just retribution.

Fourier had no doubt discussed these views in cafés and had heard many of the arguments outlined above. In any case he uses them all in his own thesis. In so far as he dissents from any of these views, he does so because they do not allow the child sufficient freedom. In his system the restraining hands of parents and teachers are removed, and children are left to find their own way.[26]

The smooth functioning of the phalange, even with the children free to do as they please, will come about through *l'entraînement ascendant*. This principle, says Fourier, is little known and much abused in civilization and yet it is of immense importance. It is the tendency of all children to imitate those slightly older and to defer to all their desires. This tendency finds pernicious expression in civilization, where the child is given little opportunity for constructive expression. The amusements of children in civilization are malicious, or dangerous, or largely useless. The 'free child' abandons himself to productive labour, thanks to the conditions provided, which will be discussed in detail later.

Fourier appreciates that important thinkers, such as Montaigne, Rollin and Rousseau, had emphasized the need to improve the relationship between the teachers and pupils. They desired to introduce greater intimacy and respect. This intention, however, says Fourier, was more laudable than judicious, for "elle est comme tant d'autres chimères incompatible avec l'ordre civilisé". This idea is impossible on two counts: first, the repugnance children have for study, and secondly, the meagre remuneration and low status of the teachers.[27]

Nature, Fourier asserts, has given the child a repugnance for the lessons given by a parent or instructor. The leaders a child will always choose for himself are children of an age one-third or one quarter older than his own. Thus, for example, "A dix-huit mois, il revère l'enfant de deux ans, et le choisit passionnément pour guide; A deux and il choisira l'enfant de trente mois; A trois ans, celui de quatre ans; A huit ans, celui de dix ans; A douze ans, celui de quinze ans."[28] He best accepts criticism from them, and is most willingly disciplined by them. This emulation, Fourier further asserts, will double its strength if the child sees his elders organized collectively, and all deriving pleasure from work and study successfully accomplished in groups.[29] Thus in the phalange children will be left to bring themselves up. Directed by the law of nature, the 'entraînement ascendant' will lead to the good of the whole community.

The organization of the life of the phalange revolves around the 'series'. The life of the growing child does likewise, and it is within these various groups that he receives his education.[30] The series, as we have seen, are groups of persons carrying or pursuing some activity. Series cater for industrial or occupational groups as well as for other social, educational and leisure activities. Children and adults may come together in a series of social service. Groups of hunters when hunting will belong to the hunters' series; but some of these same people later in the day while cooking will belong to the cooking group and series. Any individual may, because of diversity of skill, occupy a humble position within say the hunters' series but yet excel as a notable chef later. In fact, the number of different and contrasted groups a person might belong to is a fair measure of his success and maturity. But Fourier was far too optimistic about the possibility of co-operation among infants and the under-tens. For as Jean Piaget has written: "It is not until ten or eleven years that group work gives the best results; children aged five to seven years tend to be egocentric; those aged eight to ten years are capable only of sporadic co-operation."[31]

Many of these groups require skilled and experienced people, and so are obliged to provide training facilities. Children are encouraged as early as they are capable of enrolling as trainees with as many groups as possible.

The aim is the absorption of children into the industrial life of the phalange as soon as possible; Fourier estimates that a child would have joined a sufficient number of such groups and so become economically self-supporting in the phalange by four and a half years of age.[32]

The attainment of position and status in a number of *occupational* groups, e.g. as dish washers, onion growers, potato peelers, leads to admittance into a *form* or *age* group. These age groups or tribes have ceremonial functions, boys and girls meet in their tribes on feast days, or inter-village rallies; but primarily they are a means of encouraging, promoting and directing the child's educational progress. These *age* groups are listed below. Fourier was never satisfied with the esoteric names he gave these various "choeurs de l'enfance"; he was forever changing them.[33]

Choeurs de l'enfance.

The division of children into 'tribes', 'forms', or 'age' groups.

Age (Approx.)	Tribe
0 – 1	Nourissons ou Allaités
0 – 2	Poupons ou Sevrés
2 – 3	Lutins et Lutines
3 – 4½	Bambins et Bambines
4½ – 6½	Chérubins et Chérubines
6½ – 9	Séraphins et Séraphines
9 –12	Lycéens et Lycéennes
12 –15½	Gymnasiens et Gymnasiennes
15½–20	Jouvenceaux et Jouvencelles

See: U. U., iv, 7, 13, 54–5.
N. M., 170, 205.
Manus. (1851), 115; (1852), 106.

A boy, say three to four and a half years, would be encouraged to accumulate all the qualifications necessary to gain promotion from his present Bambin tribe to the next up in the scale, the Cherubins. This would entail passing a variety of tests, and showing evidence of experience within a number of *occupational* groups. Fourier emphasizes the necessity of giving a wide choice and the need to set a standard well within the child's level of development and ability. The primary task is to develop a scheme which will give *all* an opportunity of excelling in a variety of different tasks and at the same time exert and stretch each individual's ability. Clearly Fourier's idea is similar to that used in modern comprehensive schools, where children in the same house or form all go off to different lessons each in accordance with his inclination and ability.[34]

The establishment of these tribes will thus give status, position and a feeling of importance and achievement to *all* children in the phalange; skill and talent in whatever sphere will receive recognition. Membership of tribes really becomes a status symbol, and their names are only relevant in so far that they distinguish the tribe from others and enhance the desirability of belonging. Fourier is very conscious of the need constantly to reassure, encourage and praise the child. He was thus constantly devising badges, medals, uniforms, ranks, orders, to bestow on all who show merit or achievement at *all* levels; and he did this also to help and encourage others to attain similar rewards. Here again, his ideas resemble those of the Boy Scout movement, where children pass numerous tests, attain second and then first class status, and where they may aspire to the titles of All Round Cord, Bushman's Thong and Queen's Scout, by attaining proficiency in a number of skills chosen from a fairly wide field. Fourier's scheme differs in principle only in that it covers industrial and academic as well as social, moral and practical training.

Fourier allows that there must be some formal instruction, and he does recognize that achievement, skill and proficiency require long training and much experience. So Fourier does go into the question of expert teachers. He sees three factors as of decisive importance in any discussion of teachers: their position and status in society, their selection and security of tenure, and their methods of teaching.[35] He is well aware that all these factors are interdependent.

Status, rank and esteem in society ought, says Fourier, to correspond with the utility of the services rendered to the community. Education, because it performs an indispensable service, without which man would find himself "ravalé fort audessous des brutes", deserves a secure and high place in the esteem of society.[36] And yet education is little esteemed in civilized society where, says Fourier, teachers are among the lowest of the low. They are reduced to beggary, while the ignorant amass large fortunes. Even in the great cities, such as

Bordeaux and Lyon, professors have little to separate them from sellers of matches. These small rewards coupled with the malicious and odious behaviour of children in civilized schools, attract only the poorest sort into the profession.

In Harmony, the services of teachers will be recognized and much respected. The methods of selection of teachers will give them increased prestige and standing within the phalange. Since pupils are entirely free to choose whom they will to instruct them in any branch of knowledge, anyone who can attract pupils may hold forth in his speciality in the manner of the Greek sophists.[37]

It would seem that teachers of high calibre, well versed in their specialities and with a considerable following will be elected into the "corps sibyllin ou corps des instituteurs".[38] This would be an honorary status akin to a fellowship of the Royal Society, carrying immense prestige but no privileges; exclusive rights of teaching would not thereby be gained. Election to the "corps sibyllin", unlike that to the Royal Society, would be by non-members. Moreover, under Fourier's scheme, there will be opportunity for attainment of high office in teaching at all levels and in all spheres, while age will be no bar.

The peculiarity of the system is that there are no full-time teachers. All within the phalange, young and old, are at liberty to pursue a dozen to some two dozen occupations simultaneously. Thus, at any stage or in any occupation, those with the urge to teach will associate with a recognized teacher, and subsequently endeavour to seek election to the "corps sibyllin".

In Harmony teaching groups will never exceed ten; teachers will thus restrict themselves to eight or ten pupils.[39] When classes exceed a dozen, as they do in civilization, teaching, says Fourier, becomes impossible: the teacher is unable to deal with the difficulties of more than a dozen pupils at a time, more than three-quarters of the class are unable to follow the lesson, and most are in any case uninterested. And yet, in Harmony, the great popularity and renown of some teachers will attract learners from far afield. Overcrowding will be avoided by the introduction of a modified system of mutual instruction or the monitorial system. The principal teacher will have under him several advanced pupils, who, instructed by the master, will in turn pass on what they have learned to those lower down the scale. These teaching tasks will, in general, only be undertaken by those aspiring to a high level of excellence, and who in their turn might wish for election into the "corps sibyllin". Thus they will not only spend some time teaching, but will also devote themselves to improving their own personal skill; and what better a way to digest and consolidate what one has learnt than teaching it! A successful teacher, a member of the sibyls, who might well attract pupils from several of the surrounding phalanstères, could have as many as sixteen assistants of varying skill and ability.[40] Fourier, always appreciative of distinctive levels of development in children, allows for extreme specialization within the "corps sibyllin". Age is immaterial, rank goes with utility: even among the bambins, it will be possible to find fully fledged 'sibyls'. All subjects are equally meritorious and the teaching of any age group is equally worthy of high esteem.

The "corps sibyllin" will thus provide a nucleus through which the "formal" diffusion of knowledge will be undertaken. They are, however, at most helpers and guides, ready to give assistance when *eagerly* and *passionately* demanded, and never under compulsion. Those who have the aptitude and desire to learn and excel will ask and voluntarily seek help. This, Fourier maintains, is in sharp contrast to the position in civilized schools. Under the mutual system, there is a firm discipline, compulsion is enforced by punishment and beating, work is set, and there is no choice of teacher. Whereas his system allows complete freedom, attendance at classes is never compulsory, and there is a free choice of subjects and teachers. Moreover, in Harmony, teachers are numerous,[41] skilled and enthusiastic specialists. All these factors, asserts Fourier, will engender between pupils and teachers "une attraction respective ou intimité".[42] This, sympathy and mutual respect between pupil and teacher, this need to introduce a favourable atmosphere conducive to learning is impossible of attainment, asserts Fourier, despite what Montaigne, Rollin and Rousseau may say, except within his own system. Fourier does not prove his case.

The method of mutual instruction "l'enseignement mutuel ou mode composé convergent", would, argues Fourier, not only radically alter the relations and status of the teacher with his pupils, but also with society. In Harmony, teaching is only one of the numerous occupations and varied interests the individual will pursue. These alternative opportunities will give teachers an interdependence and freedom which Fourier maintains will be in sharp contrast to the slavery and misery of the civilized pedagogue.

Fourier's conception of professionalism emphasizes the vocational aspect. Work ought to be pleasant, interesting and rewarding, and so he stresses the need for teachers to engage in their work from a sense of vocation and out of interest. Moreover, the provision of alternative occupations and training within the phalange makes it extremely easy for unsuitable, tired or disillusioned teachers to give up when they feel so inclined.

The problem of movement between different occupations is, of course, currently important in our rapidly changing industrial society, but it is particularly pertinent to the teaching profession which is expanding so rapidly. As Professor Langeveld has written: "What a school system needs is not only an entrance for the teacher but also an emergency exit . . . If the teaching profession [were] open in order to have a better social circulation, teachers may come in and bring with them the fresh air of another social experience. Similarly, the teacher who is less successful should be able to move out of the profession. It is helpful when the community has other places available for the man or woman with a teaching certificate. If teachers are trained in such a way that they become specialists who can only survive in a given school system, they will be resolute opponents of any kind of change and will cling to that system to their last breath."[43] The advantages of Fourier's system is that the teacher would maintain an *active* contact with many different fields of activity, and mobility between occupations will be easy. The position of the teacher in the phalange would be perhaps more analogous to that of a voluntary social worker, Scoutmaster, or Sunday School teacher. His active participation in several different spheres would prevent the growth of "sociological and psychological" barriers described by R. J. Havighurst and B. L. Neugarten.[44] In the phalange, the teacher would no longer feel, as he so commonly does now, socially isolated and underprivileged, in fact, a "sociological stranger".[45]

This is in accord with Fourier's principles, for he is aware that "As is the school, so is society. And as is the teacher, so is the school."[46] But he goes further, for teacher, school and society are for him intensively linked, almost inseparable in identity. Education for Fourier is through active living. And so, as we have seen, the educative role of children is acknowledged and indeed valued by Fourier. He does not underestimate the importance or authority of the positions held by the youngsters who lead their peers. Boys and girls in our own time occupying positions such as sixers, patrol leaders, monitors, football or cricket captains, etc. would within the phalange be eligible for election to the "corps sibyllin". Later as they grow up some still imbued with the desire to render social service may well become the equivalent of Scoutmasters, first-aid instructors, or assume innumerable other roles. Election into the "corps sibyllin" will follow on several occasions and presumably any expert may qualify, provided he is sufficiently endowed, to teach more than one subject.

The idea of part-time teaching by highly qualified experts intent on instructing their particular speciality is most interesting and valuable. This method of teaching might well be developed, with suitable modifications, in our schools. There is no reason why experts should not come and explain their, albeit highly specialized, work, in schools, or better still why pupils should not go into the factories and business houses to receive their instruction on the spot. Any tradesman, farmer, or other worker need only make his contribution once a year, and need only spend a comparatively short time with his learners. This will be in accord with Fourier's dictum of short but attractive and interesting sessions. It may bring variety and interest to the worker and more than likely improve his status and self respect. Moreover, especially if carefully selected, the practitioner may well illuminate much that the teacher can only partly explain.

This type of instruction, first suggested by Fourier, is slowly developing and finding a formal place in the curriculum of many schools. The reassessment of the position of the part-time teacher in our schools and colleges is likewise slowly giving rise to a system which may well have a striking similarity to the "corps sibyllin" first vaunted by Fourier.[47]

1. *Republic*, Book v; see R. R. Rusk, *The Doctrines of the Great Educators* (1954), 28.
2. U. U., i, 211–12.
3. Gray, op. cit., 192.
4. See Chapter 8.
5. Q. M., 131.
6. *Emile*, Payne's ed., 15.
7. N. M., 170 and 186.
8. U. U., iv, 300–1.
9. Cp. *Emile*, Payne's ed., 15. "As the real nurse is the mother, the real preceptor is the father."
10. N. M., 175.
11. U. U., iv, 201–3.
12. U. U., iv, 204.
13. U. U., iv, 204.
14. *Republic*, Book v.
15. *Politics*, ii.
16. "Whether this was because the family was no longer a threat, whether the authorities decided that family ties were too strong to break, whether it seemed better to acknowledge the family as the primary group to be federated into larger units, or whether it was the rise in juvenile delinquency that was convincing" is not clear, but "the fact remains that since then the closeness of families has been acknowledged". M. Waddington, in *Communist Education* (1963), 55.
17. E. Westermarck: *The future of Marriage in Western civilization* (1936), 157.
18. For a detailed discussion see e.g. Dr. H. Darin-Drabkin, *The Other Society* (1962).
19. John Bowlby, "Children in the Kibbutz", *The Guardian*, 3 July 1963.
20. U. U., iv, 291.
21. For an account of English developments see H. C. Barnard, *A History of English Education from 1760* (1961), 52–7.
22. M. Gontard, *L'Enseignement Primaire en France* (1959), 282. Many famous names were associated with its foundation: Ampère, the economist J.-B. Say, Lafayette, Saint-Simon, Carnot, Chateaubriand, Guizot, La Rochefoucauld-Liancourt and others.
23. See Gontard, op. cit., 277–85.
24. D. Salmon, *Joseph Lancaster*, 7, quoted by Barnard, op. cit., 53.
25. Quoted by Gontard, op. cit., 279.
26. The removal of restraints and the reliance on the child's desires and needs is, similarly, a characteristic of the educational systems of Homer Lane and A. S. Neill. Homer Lane, *Talks to Parents and Teachers* (1954); E. T. Bazeley, *Homer Lane and the Little Commonwealth* (1948). There are many other similarities between the ideas of Fourier and Neill. See e.g. *The Free Child* (1953); *Summerhill: A Radical Approach to Education* (1962).
27. Manus. (1852), 248; U. U., iv, 292.
28. N. M., 187.
29. N. M., 187.

30. "A partir de l'age de cinq ans, en régime sociétaire, l'enfant s'instruira lui-même, dans les réunions scientifiques et industrielles." N. M., 201.
31. *Encyclopédie Française*, vol. 15, 28. 11.
32. This point is referred to again later.
33. Cp. Manus. (1851), 115; U. U., iv, 7, 13, 14.
34. Cp. *London Comprehensive Schools: A survey of sixteen schools* (1961); R. Pedley, *The Comprehensive School* (1963).
35. U. U., iv, 273.
36. U. U., iv, 274.
37. U. U., iv, 276.
38. Saint-Just, likewise, advocated a system of elections for teachers. See *Fragmens sur les institutions républicaines* (1793), 49.
39. U. U., iv, 294.
40. U. U., iv, 295.
41. U. U., iv, 295.
42. U. U., iv, 292.
43. "The Psychology of Teachers and the Teaching Profession", *Year Book of Education* (1963), 402.
44. *Society and Education* (1957), 381 seq.
45. J. Kob, "The Teacher in an Industrial Society", *Year Book of Education* (1963), 393.
46. Mallinson, op. cit., 116.
47. Cp. Professor Dobinson's proposals for the utilization of "Academic help in schools". See *Schooling 1963–1970*, 106–7, where he writes, "In any case there is everything to be gained and nothing to be lost by involving a greater number of persons in the work of education." See also the Plowden Report, *Children and their Primary Schools* (1967).

CHAPTER FIVE

Education and Care During Infancy: a Period for the Discovery of Vocation

THE IMPORTANCE of the education of the very young was recognized by several of the great thinkers of the seventeenth and eighteenth centuries. Thus J. V. Andreae in his *Christianopolis* (1619) and J. A. Comenius in his *School of Infancy* (1663) both discuss the training of infants, but they and later writers, notably Rousseau and Pestalozzi, viewed infant education up to the age of six as the training of children within the home.[1] Influenced by Rousseau and Pestalozzi, Froebel was the first great educator on the Continent "who endeavoured to provide a coherent scheme of infant education based on the nature of the child in order to improve and supplement the training given by the mother and the nurse".[2]

Robert Owen had established his infant school at New Lanark in 1816, to enable the children of his factory employees to be looked after while their parents were at work. These were admitted at the age of three, and later two. Although they were well looked after, and ample provision was made for their mental and physical welfare, nevertheless they remained the responsibility of the parents, and went home every evening.

Under the ancien régime Mably and particularly Morelly advocated a state-controlled system of communal education in which all children were brought up together irrespective of their birth or fortune. This had in part inspired the Lepeletier plan for communal education in boarding establishments to be set up by the State. But both Morelly[3] and Lepeletier had been content to let the mother look after the child until he attained the age of five years. Lepeletier, however, did suggest in his plan that mothers were to be given encouragement, help and instruction to assist them to eliminate misery, prejudice and negligence.[4]

Fourier firmly believes that education must begin at birth. From birth the child should be brought up by the community in the company of all the other children of the phalange. In his system, the child will remain in the care of the phalange until four and a half, when he will become self-supporting.

Rousseau had, Fourier admits, seen the inadequacy of the system of education current in his time. He was, however, handicapped by his misunderstanding of the laws of association. He had illusions about the simple nature of man and the sacred duty of motherhood.[5] Consequently, "ces verbiages pompeux substituèrent de nouveaux abus à d'anciens abus".[6] Fourier acknowledges the merits of Rousseau's criticism of current educational practice, but he points out that Rousseau's *Emile* deals with a family which has an income of 50,000 francs and a dozen valets at their service. In Fourier's opinion, therefore, Rousseau is neither relevant nor adequate for the education of the masses as a whole.[7]

In Association the most opulent mother, even were she a princess, would never think of bringing up her child isolatedly in her own apartments.[8] It is true that, with the existence of perfect liberty in all relations, the mother could, if she so desired, bring up her own child, but says Fourier, none would; for none could bestow even a quarter of the care which would be bestowed upon all children, rich and poor, in the phalange. The richest mother, with every outlay at her disposal, could not have a nursery of so uniform a temperature, with elastic mats, and the company of other children of the same character, who would mutually divert and amuse each other. It is in the provision of education that the differences between civilization and harmony will be most apparent; and it is particularly in the education of early infancy that "on reconnaîtra combien le plus riche potentat civilisé est audessous des moyens de bien-être que l'Harmonie prodigue au plus pauvre des hommes et des enfants".[9]

In spite of all that is preached about the sacred duties of Nature, there is not a married couple who are not more or less tired of the cares which infants require, of the filthy and repugnant services which their weaknesses demand.[10] The segregation of children in the phalange will thus enable parents to live peaceful and unmolested lives, free from worry, especially if they realize how well cared for their children will be. In civilization the household is so arranged as to enable an infant to torment the entire establishment.[11] Infancy, being less provided with reason than mature age, insists more strongly upon the satisfaction of its instincts, for the gratification of which no means exist in civilization. The infant protests, by its cries, against its subjection to a system contrary to nature—cries which are annoying to the parent and hurtful to the child.[12] Fourier speaks from personal experience: "Je vois, au moment où j'écris, un enfant qui depuis deux mois harcèle et tient sur les dents cinq à six personnes. Trois domestiques ne suffisent pas à servir les caprices que de sots parents lui ont crées: il pousse des cris perpétuels, sans maladie. Les gouvernantes engagées pour le service de cet antechrist renonécent, perdent patience au bout d'une quinzaine."[13]

In Harmony this holding to ransom of a whole household will be impossible. Associative education, says Fourier, in satisfying fully the infant, will relieve the parents, and make two beings contented, who previously were discontented.[14] The child, Fourier asserts, desires instinctively the arrangements, comforts, and satisfactions which it would find in the nurseries of the phalange,[15] and it is only for the want of them that it distracts by its cries parents, servants and neighbours, while it injures its own health.

"Je connais si peu les instincts des petits enfants", Fourier admits, "et j'ai tant d'aversion pour cette classe d'êtres désolants, que je ne me hasarderai pas à prononcer sur leurs convenances décrites en détails: mais je puis juger la question abstractivement."[16] It must be emphasized, however, that it is not merely because of their noisy and irritable ways that Fourier would segregate children from their parents. Fourier, a confirmed bachelor, believes that the whole concept of marriage is at fault. Marriage is, for him, a source of hypocrisy, friction between the sexes,[17] extreme egotism and gives rise to antisocial behaviour.[18] Even in the cradle the child can suffer immense and irretrievable harm: family influence will tend to stifle and twist his natural growth.[19] Fourier ignores the child's need for the tender care of his own mother particularly in his first year[20] and his need for the security of the family circle.

Whether in fact even under the most modern conditions a child would be better brought up in a residential nursery seems doubtful. Where residential nurseries are in existence, as for example, for orphans, or for the children of Israeli co-operative settlers, their continuance is decided in the main by social and economic needs and not on the basis of psychological requirements. Writing of their experience of residential nurseries during the War, Dorothy Burlingham and Anna Freud claim that "there are realms in the infant's life where the residential nursery can be very helpful by creating, very much on the lines of the nursery school, excellent conditions for development (health, hygiene, development of skills, early social responses). There are . . . other realms, where it is important for residential nurseries to recognize their limitations (emotional life, character-development)."[21]

Fourier, however, sees no reason why any difficulty should arise. The attendants, he asserts, attracted and specially trained for the tasks, will exercise constant supervision and satisfy all the children's needs and desires. The mother will have no other function but to suckle the baby, and this task once fulfilled she will be free to indulge in industrial and other activities. She may even, if she so desired, absent herself for a day, for there will always be present nurses, temperamentally suitable and similar, to give the milk to the baby. Since every care will be given to all children in the nurseries, their mothers will soon realize that there is nothing their children lack. While the father, now devoid of responsibility, will be able to indulge his natural function of spoiling his children without damage to their character, since they will be protected from excessive flattery and conceit by the criticism of their peers.

Specially constructed buildings will house the babies born in the phalange. Until four and a half, the children will live communally and remain the responsibility of the entire phalange.[22] Early infancy, which extends to the age of two years, comprises the classes of children: Sucklings (Nourissons) and Weaned (Poupons). Each in turn is subdivided into three temperamental groups, without distinction of sex.

The Quiet or Good-natured.
The Restless or Noisy.
The Turbulent or Intractable.[23]

EDUCATION AND CARE DURING INFANCY

Each age group has its own 'sémistère' or nursery. Each nursery will contain three halls, for the three kinds of characters; adjacent noise-proof dormitories, as well as adjoining rooms for the nurses and doctors.[24]

Civilization, with its 'simple' and defective methods, provides only a cradle for the child as a place of repose: Association, whose system is 'compound', furnishes the child, in addition to the cradle, with an elastic mat. These mats are suspended from frames about four feet high; the children can lie and roll upon them, but are separated from each other by silken nets.[25] These nets do not prevent them from moving freely, and from seeing the other children around them, whom they can approach but cannot touch. The nursery is kept sufficiently warm, thus enabling the child to be lightly dressed, and to dispense with the heavy swaddling clothes then used. The cradles are moved by a mechanical contrivance, so that twenty can be rocked at once. A child will perform this work, normally the work of twenty women.[26]

Fourier repeatedly emphasizes the importance of never changing the passions of infants but rather allowing them full development. This can best be achieved, he says, by placing them in the company of children of sympathetic character. Infants will moreover, says Fourier, become manageable by being classed with their fellows. The noise of infants will be very much diminished in the nurseries of the phalange. The most noisy, Fourier believes, will cease their cries when placed with a dozen other little creatures, as perverse as themselves. They will silence each other by their screams, something like bullies, who become perfectly mild and abandon their overbearing conduct when they are in the company of their equals.[27] Varied diversions and amusements may, in addition, be necessary to quieten the brawlers. It remains, he says, for the nurses to discover these. Stimulated as they will be by competition, rival methods will emerge ("par lutte cabalistique et rivalité des systèmes"). The nurses will soon—in approximately a month he estimates—ascertain what will be most effective and thus put an end to the infants' incessant screams.[28]

The education of the body and the development of physical and manipulative skill is of primary importance from the earliest years. Hence the elastic mats. The exclusive use of one hand or arm, which renders the other awkward and in part useless, will for example be avoided. In civilization too, the toes are rendered useless; in Harmony, they will be so trained as to be as useful as the fingers: "par exemple une orgue harmonienne aura des claviers pour les doigts de pied; et l'organiste enfourché sur une selle, traillera des doigts de pieds presque autant que de ceux de main. If fera du talon le service des pédales que nous faisons du pied."29

The greatest care also must be taken in developing all the senses. A correct ear for music will also be given to children by singing trios and quartets three or four times a day in the nurseries, and by teaching those who are old enough to march to the sound of instruments. Methods will also be employed to add acuteness of hearing to the ability to distinguish pitch at all levels, and so give the child "the delicacy of hearing of the rhinoceros and the cossack!" The other senses must be developed and exercised in an equal degree.30

In civilization, health education is neglected: the child grows up to know little about his body and almost nothing on how to keep it in the best condition or how to look after his teeth. The bourgeois families are too busy making money to have the time to look after their children's teeth and health. This will be otherwise in Harmony. Medical attention will be available from the earliest years: the infants will be visited twice daily by the doctors of the phalange. While with a life expectancy of some one hundred and forty-four years, nothing will be more precious than a beautiful and good set of teeth. Also perfect digestion, says Fourier, is dependent upon thorough mastication and efficient teeth will be invaluable with five meals a day to take care of.

The doctors of the phalange will be specialists in preventive medicine: their interest is to see that no one falls ill. In Harmony, doctors (and dentists) will always work as a team in a group. They will be collectively remunerated in proportion to the general health of the phalange, and not according to the number of ailments or number of patients treated. Their task is consequently to maintain the phalange in good health: the fewer the number of those in need of medical attention the higher the doctors' remuneration. Moreover, to discourage malingering, acceptance of personal rewards by the doctors will be considered anti-social and dishonourable.³¹ Dentists too will be remunerated according to similar principles. As soon as the teeth appear, the infant will be visited by the dentists of the phalange, who will look after them and see that they do not deteriorate.³²

The development of industrious habits and their application to productive labour is, as we have seen, one of Fourier's primary aims for education. He would have this developed from as early an age as possible. He suggests that the discovery of the child's vocation and its development ought to begin at two years of age, in fact, as soon as the child can walk and run about.³³

Nature endows every child, says Fourier, with a great number of primary instincts and it is the task of education to discover them. These instincts, in civilization, lie dormant or are entirely smothered. So as soon as the child can walk it is taken by the 'Bonnins' and 'Bonnines'³⁴ round all the nearby workshops and industrial meeting places, where it is given ample opportunity for observation. Moreover (and this is fundamental) whenever appropriate, there will be a parallel industry in miniature with diminutive tools specially adapted for use by youngsters.

In Association little children of two and a half to three years are already at work, and these the newcomer will be anxious to join. The phalange practising as it does an exceedingly great variety of occupations, it will be almost impossible for a child passing from one to another not to find opportunities for satisfying several of his dominant instincts; these will exhibit themselves at the sight of the little tools manipulated by other children a few months older than himself.³⁵ He will rummage about, handle things, and at the end of a fortnight it may be possible to discern what are the workshops that attract him, and what are his industrial instincts. All this activity by the infant goes to show that it is not true, as civilized parents and teachers maintain, that children are little idlers. But, if they are to become ardent, enthusiastic workers, it is necessary not only to know how to attract them to industry³⁶ but also how to maintain alive the interest once it has been aroused. To do this it is first necessary to appreciate their fundamental tastes and to utilize them appropriately. The dominant tastes in all children, says Fourier,³⁷ are:

1. *Rummaging*, or inclination to handle everything, examine everything, look through everything, and constantly change occupations.
2. Industrial *commotion*, the taste for noisy occupations.
3. *Aping*, or imitative mania.
4. Industrial *miniature*, a taste for miniature workshops.
5. *Progressive attraction* of the weak towards the strong.

"Il en est bien d'autres", he admits, but he confines himself to these.

All these tastes are used in his educational schemes; but particularly, the aping or imitative mania is fundamental in Fourier's educational method. This is the wish to try what children older than themselves are doing. It is upon this fancy, termed ascending tone, that almost the entire system of attractive education, says Fourier, will be grounded.[38]

Fourier realizes that it is not merely sufficient to provide the apparatus for discovery and development of industrial vocations; nor does he believe that the child will easily emulate his more endowed companions. Positive efforts must be made to encourage him to do so. The atmosphere must be conducive to work and to self-improvement. The tools, workshops and work must be attractive in the extreme. The atmosphere must be gay and happy. And, very important, the sessions should be short, frequently varied, and animated by rivalry. Things, says Fourier, are more valued if they do not occur frequently.[39]

The best incentive for the child commencing its industrial career, says Fourier, is impartial criticism. This it never receives from the father or mother, who praise at this early stage even its faults. This indiscreet flattery will be counteracted in Association; children among themselves show no feeling but ridicule without mercy an awkward associate and dismiss it with disdain. Turned away by older children, it will go crying to its mentor, who will give it lessons and present it again, when it has acquired sufficient skill. The degree of perseverance Fourier expects is no doubt exaggerated. But Fourier is an optimist and argues that as some easy and trifling work is always reserved for this age, the child soon obtains admission to a dozen groups, in which its education progresses rapidly, "car on n'apprend vite et bien que ce qu'on apprend par attraction".[40]

The provision of tools and of miniature workshops is an

"amorce naturelle à l'industrie".⁴¹ The mania for rummaging so dominant in a child of two must be exploited. The child will persist, says Fourier, if the work coincides with any of his instincts. The patriarchs who are always about ready to help will teach him any portion of the work. The child will thus soon be acquainted with some skill—trifling no doubt—but this will enable him to be useful. These little tasks will act as introductions to industrial activity: it is of course true that they all could be completed in less time and more efficiently by an older person, but the benefit to the child and the community will be greater even when done less efficiently by the child himself.

An example Fourier gives is the shelling and sorting of peas.⁴² In the phalange, this work will be given to children of two, three and four years of age instead of to adults. A specially inclined table with a number of hollows is provided. Two infants will be seated at the raised side: they will take the peas out of the shell and arrange for them to roll down the inclined table. At the lower side three infants, aged twenty-five, thirty, thirty-five months, will sort out the peas, furnished with special implements: the smallest peas for the sweetened ragout, the medium ones for the bacon ragout and the largest for the soup. The child of thirty-five months first selects the little ones which are the most difficult to pick out; it sends all the large and medium ones to the next hollow, where the child of thirty months shoves those that seem large to the third hollow, returns the little ones to the first, and drops the medium grains into the basket. The infant of twenty-five months, placed at the third hollow, has an easy task; it returns some medium grains to the second, and gathers the large ones into its own basket.

The infant débutant placed as it ought to be in the third rank, says Fourier, will mingle proudly with the others in throwing the large grains into the basket. Although it is very trifling work, the infant will feel part of a team and that its contribution is as great as that of his companions. The infant will grow enthusiastic and be seized by a spirit of emulation, and at the third session (séance) it will be able to replace the infant of thirty-five months.⁴³ This type of child participation in the work of the phalange Fourier considers imperative. It is uneconomic but it is nevertheless an essential bait to the child and an indispensable method for enticing his co-operation.

76 THE EDUCATIONAL IDEAS OF CHARLES FOURIER

Fourier considers that the phalange must continually develop means for pupil participation in industry; for it is through actual industrial experience commensurate with age and degree of development that vocations are discovered. Thus in all branches of industry some trifling occupations should be left for childhood as a means of initiation into productive activity.

If civilized education, Fourier says, developed in every child his natural inclinations, then rich children would nearly all find their true vocation in very plebeian occupations, those of mason, carpenter, smith or saddler. Fourier cites in support of his assertion: Louis XVI, who loved the trade of a locksmith; an Infanta of Spain, who preferred that of shoemaker; a King of Denmark, who enjoyed manufacturing syringes; the King of Naples, who loved to sell the fish he had caught in the market place himself; the Prince of Parma, whom Condillac had trained in metaphysical subtleties, in the understanding of intuition and cognition, but who had no taste other than for the occupation of church-warden and lay-brother. The great majority of wealthy children would follow these plebeian tastes if civilized education did not prevent the development of them and if the filthiness of the workshops and the coarseness of the workmen did not arouse in them a repugnance stronger than attraction. What child, asks Fourier, has no taste for the occupation of mason, carpenter, smith and saddler? And would he not wish to participate in them if he beheld from an early age the work carried on in bright workshops, by refined people, who would always arrange a miniature workshop for children, with little implements, and light labour.[44]

The discovery of vocations is the primary task of the Lutinarian period, and so Fourier believes that by the time the child is three years old, and ready to join the Bambin (the first of the sixteen tribes), its industrial tendencies would have revealed themselves. Here the first distinctions between the sexes will be made,[45] but occupations are always open to talent and are never decided by sex prejudice or parental wishes.

The growth of the child, during his period of membership of the Bambins, will be continually fostered and his adherence to productive labour further encouraged. He will consolidate his vocational aspirations—these should be at least twenty in number. As he grows up he will attempt tasks previously out of his reach. There are, Fourier admits, branches of industry that a child will be unable to tackle until his tenth or even fifteenth year, hence the importance of the gimblettes harmoniques— industrial and horticultural activity, using miniature equipment, especially adapted to the different ages and abilities.[46] The various playthings always provided in the phalange are used for instructional purposes. The dog-carts, drums and dolls, for example, are used to emulate real life situations but at the level of the child's stage of development.[47]

The multiplicity of activity in the phalange enables the child to develop fully and at his own rate. To move up, within the tribes, the child will need to pass a variety of tests. All are encouraged to move up as soon as they may. The precocious child is a figure of admiration and emulation in the phalange; whereas, in civilization, Fourier says, he is a cause of envy and jealousy. Promotion up the scale of tribes is by accomplishment and examination. The principles are the same whether for the Bambin or Gymnasts. Examination is by the members of the tribe (in the particular series) to which admission is sought: children, says Fourier, are their own severest critics. There will be a wide variety of skills in which proficiency may be attained, but only a certain number need be secured before privileges of membership are granted. Fourier is emphatic that each of the seven "corporations de lutin, bambins, cherubins, seraphins, lycéens, gymnasiens et jouvenceaux" should have very carefully graded tests. Each group will award its own badges and insignia for the diverse industrial occupations. The badges and insignia awarded will be carefully graded showing the degree of accomplishment and skill, viz. "aspirant, néophyte, bachelier, licencié, officiers divers" in the particular occupation.[48] The acquisition of these honours by the child will be a particularly powerful stimulant and they will always be awarded with much ceremony during parades of the whole phalange.[49]

Fourier does not develop in any detail the contents of the various tests. He merely lists them in U. U., iv, 9, without much explanation.[50] He does, however, in his N. M., 196–7, elaborate in some respects. A child of three years will already have, he says, at least "une vingtaine de dignités et décorations, comme celles de

Licencié au groupe des allumettes
Bachelier au groupe d'égoussage
Néophyte au groupe du réséda, etc., etc.,

avec ornements de toutes ces fonctions". He cites, as another example, a Bambine, aged four and a half, a candidate for admission to the Cherubins; "Elle subira à peu près les épreuves suivantes:

1. Intervention musicale et chorégraphique à l'Opéra.
2. Lavage de 120 assiettes en une demi-heure, sans en fêler aucune.
3. Pellage d'un demi-quintal de pommes en temps donné, sans en retrancher au-delà de tel poids indiqué.
4. Triage parfait de telle quantité de riz ou d'autre grain en temps fixé.
5. Art d'allumer et couvrir le feu avec intelligence et célérité.

En outre, on exigera d'elle des brevets de licenciée dans cinq groupes, de bachelière dans sept groupes, de néophyte dans neuf groupes.

"Ces épreuves, dont le choix est libre pour la postulante, sont exigées lorsqu'elle veut monter de choeur en choeur; on en exige d'autres pour monter d'échelon en échelon, comme de bas cherubins aux mi-cherubins, etc."

The tribes, even the very youngest, say Fourier, are full of self-respect and will only admit candidates who reach the required standard. Nevertheless, if after persevering for six months, the child was still below standard, he could obtain admittance to the "choeurs de demi-caractère".[51] He would thus obtain promotion to the next tribe in this special category. This, says Fourier, will enable late developers to attain the highest possible ranks at a later stage of their careers. Fourier seems to have produced this category as an afterthought in his *Nouveau Monde*, for in *Unité Universelle*[52] he classified those unable to obtain admission to the Cherubin as idiots or "du moins des êtres subalternes". These would join the auxiliary tribe, but with the creation of the semi-character he has left room for late development. In any case, Fourier is careful to emphasize that the acceptance of a "demi-caractère", although hardly flattering, is not offensive or injurious. This class will contain

EDUCATION AND CARE DURING INFANCY 79

many individuals distinguished in other directions—possibly with highly-developed tastes for food, artistic tendencies, or high degree of intelligence which cannot be classified. It will also contain those not so well endowed.[53]

All this will take place in an environment, Fourier is continually at pains to emphasize, of absolute freedom. Full liberty of choice and duration of occupation is allowed. Perfect independence is the rule and obedience to superiors is only required if these have been freely chosen. Yet this complete freedom does not imply unregulated licence to indulge in activities dangerous to themselves or to their companions. It would be folly, says Fourier, for example to allow a seven-year-old the use of firearms, or a five-year-old the use of an axe. Children may seek pleasure where they will and do what they please, always provided it is without "danger, pour eux, et ne lèse point les convenances d'un autre corporation d'enfants. S'il plaisait à un [bambin, un] cherubin, d'arracher les fleurs cultivées par un groupe de seraphins, il y aurait lésion et motif de repression." But, asserts Fourier dogmatically, because of their education this wrong-doing, this vandalism "ne pourraient se rencontrer que chez un enfant arrivant de civilization et jamais chez ceux élevés dès le bas age en Association".[54]

Fourier's conception of infant education is rather limited and narrow, and his account is hardly comprehensive. Nevertheless his ideas are interesting and suggestive. Fourier's chronological desiderata must be ignored, since he has little idea of the relationship of chronological age with the mental, manual and social stages of development. His emphasis on the need for material and physical necessities, and on the early development and exercise of the physical and sensual faculties was certainly justified and important, particularly at the time when he was writing. His suggestions for the need to discover vocational talent and aptitude, systematically and over a period of time, are increasingly justifying themselves in the two year 'cycle d'observation' in many French schools. The need for educational guidance for our own secondary school pupils has also been cogently emphasized by Professor Dobinson.[55] Fourier's proposals for the inculcation of a love of labour and the desire for work within a group are continuing to find independent expression in the pedagogical experience of the Soviet Union. The similarities of aim and method with the Soviet Nursery school are interesting; the account given by Vera Fediaevsky of their practice in the 1930s reveals many parallels.[56] In her account, the aims of infant education are almost identical: education must: i, begin at birth, ii, prepare children to be citizens of a 'new society', iii, attention must be given to all aspects of the personality of the child, i.e. education of the whole child.[57] Stimulation of interest in the life of the community and in different tools and mechanical things is emphasized.[58] Provision is also made for older children to "assist with the distribution of bibs, or to examine the cleanliness of their younger playmates, and they also water and care for the flowers".[59] There are also supervised occupational activities, such as housekeeping, music, claymoulding.[60] Labour education is stressed; there are opportunities for the observation of and participation in adult work[61] and for the use of simple tools.[62] Political education is, of course, not neglected; "by accustoming children to play and work cooperatively we lay the foundations of the first habits of collective work".[63]

Fourier's idea of a period of two years devoted to the discovery of the child's interests and aptitudes, followed by a further period of experimental consolidation, has a parallel also in the French Langevin Plan—though there naturally this period was postponed to the early teens—and in Berthoin's two-year 'observation' classes where the child's suitability for further education was explored.[64] Vocational guidance has now become one of the principal purposes of French schools in the eleven to fifteen age range (known as "the phase of orientation").

1. Report of C. C. on *Infant and Nursery Schools* (1933); R. R. Rusk, *History of Infant Education* (1951).
2. Ibid., 1. Fourier does not appear to have known Froebel's work.
3. *Code de la nature* (1755), 314.
4. J. Guillaume, P.-V. *Convention Nationale*, vol. 2, 38.
5. U. U., iv, 47; cf. 50, 61, and N. M., 170.
6. U. U., iv, 47.
7. U. U., iv, 50.
8. U. U., iv, 52.
9. U. U., iv, 53.
10. U. U., iv, 63.
11. U. U., iv, 53.

12. U. U., iv, 65.
13. U. U., iv, 53.
14. U. U., iv, 65. Cp. "Ainsi, jusque chez l'enfance on retrouve cette fâcheuse propriété de la civilization (see also ii, 27) engendrer le double mal, au lieu du double bien que nous distinait la nature." (See also ii, 183.)
15. U. U., iv, 53.
16. U. U., iv, 64.
17. "Opinion des hommes sur le mariage, dont la grande majorité s'écrie: "Quelle folie, quelle galère que ce mariage; ah, si c'était à refaire on ne m'y prendrait plus!" U. U., iii, 75.
18. Q. M., 185.
19. N. M., 170.
20. Anna Freud, *Introduction to Psycho-Analysis for Teachers* (1949), 26; also J. A. Hadfield, *Childhood and Adolescence* (1962).
21. *Infants without Families. The case for and against Residential Nurseries* (1944), 107.
22. N. M., 171.
23. N. M., 171.
24. N. M., 171.
25. Fourier gives no further details about the exact nature and function of these nets or mats. Cp. Saint-Just, *Fragmens sur les institutions républicaines*, p. 48, "Les enfants . . . couchent sur les nattes et dorment huit heures." He does not elaborate.
26. U. U., iv, 51.
27. U. U., iv, 58.
28. U. U., iv, 59.
29. N. M., 177.
30. N. M., 176.
31. U. U., iv, 51–2.
32. U. U., iv, 66–7.
33. N. M., 180.
34. See Chapter 4.
35. U. U., iv, 28.
36. N. M., 180.
37. N. M., 181.
38. U. U., iv, 28.
39. N. M., 184.
40. N. M., 186.
41. N. M., 182.
42. N. M., 182.
43. N. M., 182.
44. U. U., iii, 543.
45. N. M., 191.
46. N. M., 193. For further details much on similar lines to the case of shelling of peas see case study of Nisus and Euryale, N. M., 193.
47. N. M., 194.
48. N. M., 195.
49. U. U., iv, 27.

50. e.g. "1° En gradation des [lutins aux bambins et des] bambins aux cherubins: sept épreuves matérielles à son choix; sept exercices de dextérité appliquée proportionnément aux diverses parties du corps . . . 4° En gradation des lycéens aux gymnasiens: on exige vingt épreuves, dont huit en matériel et douze en spirituel, avec thèse pivotale sur l'unité de système de Dieu en régie d'univers."
51. N. M., 198.
52. U. U., iv, 13.
53. N. M., 198.
54. U. U., iv, 21.
55. *Schooling 1963–70* (1963), 18.
56. *Nursery School and Parent Education in Soviet Russia* (1936).
57. Ibid., 82–3.
58. Ibid., 88–9.
59. Ibid., 70.
60. Ibid., 93.
61. Ibid., 96.
62. Ibid., 97.
63. Ibid., 101.
64. For details of these plans see V. Mallinson, "Development of the idea of the Ecole Unique in France", *Forum*, ii, 3 (1960), 112–14.

CHAPTER SIX

Five to Ten Years

FOURIER assumes, as we have just seen, that by four and a half years, the vocations and abilities of the child would have been discovered.[1] The child has found those occupations which attract him and for which he has a natural affinity. The organization of the phalange now enables him to join in those industrial activities and so attain economic independence.

Fourier is perhaps excessively eager to make the child self-supporting as early as possible; but on this count he does not differ from most of his contemporaries. In England, at the time, children in their thousands, according to Robert Owen, were generally admitted into the cotton mills " . . . some at five, many at six, and a greater number at seven", and worked "sixteen hours a day whenever the trade went well".[2] Conditions in the French factories and mills were not dissimilar; there too children and adolescents suffered greatly.[3]

Although Fourier insists upon the child's economic independence, he maintains that the child is as yet otherwise undeveloped. According to Fourier, he is capable of undertaking simple manual tasks which cover his upkeep but his physical powers, manual dexterity, and vocational aptitudes remain yet to be fully developed and utilized. Likewise, the emotional and social aspects of his personality need time and opportunity to grow and evolve. These varied aspects are interdependent but predominate, according to Fourier, in varying degrees through childhood and adolescence. The five–ten years period is primarily a time when the child seeks satisfaction through his senses; hence at this time the development of the *material* (bodily) aspect is paramount.[4] During this, the five–ten years, phase of education the emphasis must be on active participation, of learning through doing.

No attempt must at this stage, says Fourier, be made to create precocious little savants, intellectual primary school beginners, initiated from their sixth year in scientific subjects. Here Fourier follows Rousseau, who likewise asserted the need to postpone purely intellectual exercise. Fourier's aim is first to secure mechanical precocity, capability in bodily industry, which he believes, far from retarding the growth of the mind, will accelerate it. He observes that children from four and a half to nine years of age are strongly drawn to all material exercises and very little to studies. The mind can hardly develop satisfactorily unless the body has first been prepared to enable it to do so. The physical development of the child is thus both an end in itself, and a preparation for the growth of the mind. Moreover, the child must be integrated into society, and so social training is important. He must thus early be found a place within the community and made to feel an increasingly valuable member and one whose assistance is generously appreciated.

The development of a perfect body and the attainment of right attitudes and sentiments towards work and the community necessitate, says Fourier, the introduction of two resources quite foreign to the civilized methods of education: the *Opera* and *Cookery*. Fourier denies that there is something arbitrary in this selection, and so far as his system is concerned it is inevitable—"méthodiquement obligé".[5]

Opera and Cookery are two focal points of "natural attraction" for the child. Children (and cats) would for ever be haunting the kitchens, if they were not chased away. Likewise, the magic fairy-land, the visible and musical enchantment of the opera is a source of perpetual delight for children.[6] This is because, says Fourier, between five and ten years, the sensitive passions dominate and are the prime motivators of behaviour. The child is strongly inclined to the enjoyment of taste, smell, sight and hearing: the first two he finds so prevalent in the kitchens and the last two dominant at the opera.

This childish inclination is apparently in accord with Nature's wishes, for man needs above all health and wealth for his happiness and mere knowledge is insufficient. And it is because of this, argues Fourier, that nature wishes man to turn first into a husbandman and manufacturer, and only later into a scientist and scholar.[7] This point is quoted with approval in a manual on

"The Principles of Communist Education" recently published in the Soviet Union.[8] Cooking and the opera are natural baits to entice the child into the adult world of the phalange.

Fourier gives the 'opera' and 'cooking' wide meaning and he intends there to be an immense variety of experience and work to be available in each. Cooking and opera will provide wide opportunities for the exercise of the four passions, as well as enable them to develop along useful and profitable lines, leading to work in the fields, kitchens, buildings, farms, and so on. Here we now discuss 'cooking' and the 'opera' in turn.

Fourier is clearly tremendously excited by the opportunities he sees in cooking as a method for education. Cooking forms a unifying directive force in the child's early educational progress. The child's attraction for the kitchen, his greed and his interest in eating[9] are all used to create an interest in cooking as well as in the growth, preparation and consumption of food. Thus Fourier links the activities of kitchen with the work of the market gardens, farms, and animals of the phalange.

Fourier sees the kitchen as an integral part of agrarian studies. He observes that "pour faire de l'enfant un parfait agronome en gestion animale et végétable, il faut de très-bonne heure l'initier aux raffinements de cette cusine, de cette gastronomie, proscrites par les farouches amis des raves et du 'brouet noir'."[10] The production of food for consumption is after all the aim of the farmer and market gardener, and, asks Fourier, how are they to judge the requirements of the cook unless they have some knowledge and training in cooking? He is particularly critical of civilized parents who lay so much emphasis on the agricultural education of their sons: knowledge of horticulture, animal husbandry, and the conservation of their products is much encouraged, but skill in cooking is ignored, and even disparaged. However, Fourier does not wish to neglect any of these: the greater the knowledge all round, the higher the standards attained.[11] An all-round training is necessary and children must be enticed to spend time in groups within the kitchen, as well as in the market gardens, and farms.

Fourier compares the position of children in civilized and harmonian kitchens. In the former, the child is discouraged or even refused entry, he finds that he is awkward and smashes the plates, and then he burns himself; he cannot handle the fire and he is even forbidden to come near it. There is no guide or instructor for the child, and no provision is made to employ the child. This is in sharp contrast with the harmonian kitchen, which is suitably equipped for use by youngsters, where the child is made welcome and found work appropriate for his age, interest and ability.

In these new-type kitchens the furniture will be so constructed and the lay-out so arranged that it will be suitable for use by both adults and children.[12] Small, specially designed stoves, miniature pots, saucepans, casseroles and other necessary utensils will make it possible for the youngsters to emulate and learn the work of the adults cooking nearby with full-sized equipment. But some of the simpler jobs, such as the peeling of potatoes or boiling beans, might be done directly by the children. Likewise, children might be found useful jobs in the pantries, the dairy, the confectionery or in the fruit and vegetable shops, all of which form an integral part of the "cuisine sériares". Fourier reckons that the confectionery will surpass the others since it is an earthly paradise for children; and inevitably it will be the first school and place of learning for the "poupons" and the "bambins".[13]

Cooking, says Fourier, is particularly conducive to the formation of groups and hence is, for him, an educative process. There are obviously innumerable degrees of skill, varied abilities and tastes, as well as much scope for innovation and imagination in cooking. The opportunities for emulation are excellent, and the desire to excel inevitably stimulated. Fourier rather optimistically believes that all this will lead to rivalry and so eventually to an improvement in skill.

This preoccupation of children with food will not, asserts Fourier, turn them into gluttons and gormandizers, for it is well known that they are that already. "Les enfants", Fourier quotes his contemporaries as saying, "sont des petits gourmands, il faut les corriger, modérer leur passions."[14] This he maintains shows a lack of understanding of the true position. In general, the most temperate class of people at meal times are the cooks. They are generally epicures,[15] severe judges, partaking indeed of all dishes, but without going to any excess.[16] The best preservation against gluttony then, says Fourier, for children as well as parents, would be an order of things where they would all become *cooks* and *refined gourmands*, otherwise called gastronomes. And so Fourier makes it one of the tasks of Associative education to produce such epicures.

Again Fourier hopes rather optimistically that interest in food will create curiosity in the ingredients required, in the vegetable produce and in animal breeding. This ought to prove an additional incentive to a child free to choose his own occupation and being at liberty to move between several in any one day, to seek and devote himself to the numerous tasks connected with horticulture and the care of animals. These activities moreover, asserts Fourier, are peculiarly suitable for children.

Two-thirds of our gardens contain little plants, shrubs and flowers which, says Fourier, are eminently suitable for cultivation by children and women. Organized in groups, the children of the phalange must therefore be made responsible for these pursuits. Fourier does not give specific details, but merely explains that experience within these groups would count towards promotion in the ranks of the childhood tribes. Moreover, he believes that in pursuance of this work in horticulture a child would acquire an elementary knowledge of the various sciences, for, says Fourier, agriculture is connected with them all. For example, a child seeking admittance to the bambins must, at its examination for promotion, show knowledge of at least one flower or vegetable, like the pansy or chervil, and prove that it has participated in the group responsible for its cultivation. A candidate for the cherubins must possess practical knowledge and skill in the cultivation of at least three vegetables as well as providing evidence of useful service within the appropriate series.[17]

Active rivalry between the phalanges will always exist, and so a group producing strawberries may find its produce declared inferior to that grown in a neighbouring phalange. The group would want to know the reasons for this misfortune. It may perhaps be due to differences in the soils. This offers an opportunity to the Mentor, directing the group, to give them a lesson on the varieties of soils; and this study perhaps continued in other groups will give them an elementary knowledge of minerals. It may be that this might even be for some an incentive to attend school and seek further enlightenment in an elementary book on the classification of soils.[18] Thus Fourier makes the point, important in his educational method, that in Association a child is never given *simple* instruction. He is initiated into any particular science, by combining that science with practical notions previously acquired in different branches of industry (but particularly at first in agriculture and the kitchen).

Agricultural rivalries will early accustom children to a speculative and investigating approach. This attitude is very necessary in the cultivation of flowers; for what is more difficult, asks Fourier, than to raise to perfection the jonquil, the narcissus, the buttercup, the tulip or the rose? If nature requires so much knowledge in the case of these flowers, it is because, Fourier asserts, she wishes to accustom the minds of children, who have a passion for their cultivation, to a habit of examination and reflection.

Nature had also reserved them some parts in the 'heavier' branches of agriculture, such as the cultivation of buckwheat, beans, peas. A group of children devoted to the cultivation of these vegetables is obliged to study the quality of the soil and manures, and to understand the influence of climate in order to comprehend the cause of the success of various phalanges. A child thus devoted to these occupations will insensibly acquire the knowledge of a chemist and a naturalist; whereas otherwise chemistry and botany might have become meaningless and boring facts learnt under compulsion.[19]

Another essential part of the education of children will be, perhaps paradoxically, their close association with the animals of the phalange. The animals of the phalange will be trained and looked after mainly by children, aged five to nine, organized in series; but older children will also help and generally supervize. These tasks will be numerous: Fourier does not enumerate them, he confines himself to saying that naturally a child of six will look after pigeons and fowl rather than cows and horses. In civilization a child can do nothing but frighten and corrupt animals; and even a dog is badly brought up.

Animals, if they are to prove profitable to man in industry, must be trained along principles of harmonious education. Only children themselves brought up on harmonious lines will successfully train animals. Fourier believes that the methods of directing animals in civilization are confused and unsatisfactory; the use of the whip, a barbaric method, is very common among the French.

Animals in Harmony will be trained to respond to music. (Here Fourier seems to anticipate the Pavlovian approach to training.) It will thus be possible with the use of bells to let the animal know what is required of it. Animals will be trained from birth to follow a particular sound, which they will also learn to associate with their food. Cows, sheep and horses will, while young and during their period of education, carry (round them) a bell emitting a given note, which they will follow for the remainder of their lives. This will suffice to distribute them into squadrons and columns. "Par exemple, pour classer et faire cheminer en bon ordre un troupeau de vingt quatre mille moutons, trois ou quatre bergers à cheval sont rangés aux extrémités et au centre, avec quelques chiens de police et huit chiens de gamme qui, au signal donné, agitent alternativement leurs colliers de sonnettes, et rallient autour d'eux les moutons élevés sur leur note. On range les sonnettes par tierce, afin que chacune s'accorde avec la suivante et la précédente . . . En Harmonie, on conduit plus aisément cinquante mille moutons qu'aujourd'hui cinq cents."[20] This musical method combined, as it will be, with attractive food, satisfactory surroundings and gentle handling, will tame a zebra, or even a beaver, as it will the horse.[21]

It is impossible, says Fourier, to discipline immense flocks without a knowledge of their language. Now if the civilized continue to stun animals with their varied and arbitrarily chosen cries, the feeble intelligence of these animals will never enable them to achieve a collective and unitary discipline or understanding. But once this diversity of usage is stopped "en congrès d'unité sphérique" animal language would become the same the world over.

It will be necessary for the Harmonian child to know how to live "unitairement" with animals, how to summon them and have a few words of command at his disposal. A child unable to make himself understood with animals will be refused admittance by the Cherubins. The Cherubinian jury will let him know that a person cannot be admitted to the ranks of the Harmonians who is as yet not the equal of animals, "puisqu'il ne sait ni leur langage, ni leur convenances".[22]

The appropriate yet gentle methods of management, the choice of variety of sustenance, the care bestowed upon them by the "sectaires", the careful precautions in regard to breeding, all these will tend to make the animals happy in Harmony. None of this can prevail, nor indeed does it prevail, in the brutalized civilization where even commodious stables are not provided. It is possible to state without exaggeration, says Fourier, that even asses in Harmony will be better lodged and better looked after than the peasants of France. This discipline and refinement of the animal kingdom will bring material advantages far superior to those possible in civilization. These economic advantages will be enormous and, says Fourier, can only be achieved through Harmonious education. The children aided by a few old folk will be responsible for these savings. These adults, named 'sibyls' and 'sibylles' will guide the children and will themselves be experts in animal care and training.[23]

We now return to the 'opera', to discuss this other important means of utilizing the two passive passions, sight and hearing, in the education of the child aged five to ten.

The opera in the phalange will be, says Fourier, a centre of activity for all, but particularly useful for the children. Its value as a medium of education had been ignored in civilization.[24] In the phalange, participation in the productions will be almost universal. Fourier is not surprised that the 'moral and religious class' disapprove of the opera, for he agrees that in civilization the opera is nothing but an arena of gallantry and an allurement to expenditure. In Harmony, it is an amicable reunion, free of charge. It cannot be the occasion of any vicious intrigues between people who meet each other frequently in the various occupations of the industrial series.[25] Children, he believes, are strongly attracted to the magic and enchantment of the opera. The opera through 'attraction' and the two passive senses—sight and hearing—will open up innumerable avenues for the cultivation of the faculties of the child.

The opera uses a variety of skills and talents. These require training and then are utilized in a co-operative venture. The individual must, in general, subordinate his contribution to the whole. The result is a combined effort of many adults and children. The production will thus necessitate immense planning and discussion, and many varied groups and sub-groups will be formed. In this, as well as in the exercise of his senses, the personality of the child will develop.

The Harmonians having, as Fourier puts it, been born as it were on the stage,[26] are motivated in their acting by enthusiasm and habit rather than self-interest. As we have seen, infants are brought up to appreciate music, as well as to sing in choirs, from their earliest days. A child of four and a half is expected to have a decently trained voice, ear and pitch—if he does not attain a reasonable degree of performance, it can but be an "estropié de naissance".[27] Each working group and series will have its own cantatas and hymns which all will intone or sing at the beginning and end of each session, "comme le Benedicité et les Grâces dans les monastères".[28] The child, thus trained and encouraged with innumerable attendances at concerts from an early age, will have his natural desire to participate in opera reinforced. There his singing will improve even more.

Children will also be encouraged to learn various musical instruments. These they will learn, and later play in the orchestra at the opera. But musicians will also be required to provide the music for the numerous parades. Fourier loved watching soldiers drilling, parading, and performing military manoeuvres. And so, "les enfants harmoniens excelleront dans toutes les manoeuvres, inconnues même des fameux cavaliers tartares, mameluks, arabes et mahrattes . . . [elles seront] en mode rectiligne et curviligne, soit en ordre serré, soit en espace, ou lâche, des manoeuvres variées à l'infini, comme celles des ballets d'opéra".[29] The basic training for participation in these they will obtain at the opera!

Speech and manner of delivery will be cultivated. The child, if he is to be successful as an actor, will have to learn to speak clearly and meaningfully. The gestures he makes, his method of expression, his carriage and deportment will all, no doubt, come under critical scrutiny. He will thus learn much.[30] In his endeavours to improve, the child will have the help and encouragement of those slightly older than himself, the members of the Little Bands.[31]

Gymnastics and the control of bodily movements is also to be learnt from participation in the opera. Fourier complains that very little gymnastics are seen at the opera and what is done is relegated to small theatres. He is critical of this and would like to see more of the "grotesques, funanbules, sauteurs, etc." for these are noble activities and give pleasure to people.³²

Painting, scenery, construction and costume design will again occupy many and give opportunity for the formation of groups for these differing activities and so, Fourier hopes, give rise to much opportunity for healthy rivalry and organization. Thus from an early age children will practise the various trades associated with production of the opera, e.g., scenery makers, painters, dressmakers and carpenters.³³

The opera also serves to promote social unity and cohesion. All classes will participate in different operas which will be produced throughout the year. Parents as well as children will be involved. Those not particularly talented will only appear perhaps two or three times in major parts, and will at other times join the chorus, orchestra, dancers, scene construction and painting groups.³⁴ A high standard of production will always prevail, for the phalange will be able to draw upon at least twelve hundred actors.³⁵ Thus each phalange will have an opera house much superior to those of Paris, London and Naples.³⁶

Opera production, says Fourier, necessitates a high degree of co-operation and individual submission to the will of the mass. Even a young prince will have to learn to dance in step and sing in unison. Consideration for others will be necessary, as will be communication. Manners will be cultivated and improved.³⁷ People will cease to boo and whistle; and the warmth of applause will suffice to inform the actor of the views of the audience. But there will be no bad actors, says Fourier, "parce que leur quantité immense oblige à chacun à se restreindre à un petit nombre de pièces où il excelle".³⁸ Since people will have to learn to understand each other, they will speak clearly. Language, in civilization a barrier between districts and classes,³⁹ will tend to uniformity. Mutual understanding will grow.

Fourier recognized that the opera was developed for the leisured class and had become in his time much of a status symbol. This is, too, a contemporary viewpoint, and it is a common question nowadays to ask whether it is possible "to spread this cultured heritage more widely without transforming and debasing it".⁴⁰ Fourier desired to utilize the opera as a means of bringing the social classes together, and imbibing them with a common social purpose. It is easy to say in civilization with some frivolous moralists "qui bien chante et bien danse, peu avance"; but in Harmony Fourier never tires of reminding his readers that the opera inculcates habits of work and an attitude of mind impossible to create otherwise. Diversion and pleasure in the opera, as in all other activities of the phalange, must be closely linked with productive labour and designed to enhance its dignity and usefulness. The contents of the opera must therefore be directed to the enhancement of the moral tone of the community. "L'opéra est une école de morale en image."[41] The type of opera, as well as its manner of presentation, is therefore a fundamental influence on the mores of the child and the community.

To sum up: Fourier sees 'cooking' and 'opera' as two complementary methods of education. The training received participating in the one benefits the other: for example, he cites the child's knowledge of music as useful in the training of animals. The two aspects are closely linked and designed, as always with Fourier, to develop the child's potentialities and direct them in the service of the community. He is emphatic that his purpose is to reverse the trends in civilization where, he maintains, recreations and diversions lead children to idleness, abandonment of work, and even crime, theft, gambling and suicide.[42] He is vitally concerned with the social environment. He sees irresponsible behaviour, 'anti-social' attitudes and juvenile delinquency as manifestations of an inadequate educational system. He endeavours to devise educational methods which will help eliminate social problems, and create a society where natural or spontaneous behaviour need not be deemed 'anti-social' but is rather pleasing and useful. His insight into social factors of education are perceptive and useful even to-day.

Similarly, Fourier's concern with activity as a basis of learning anticipated modern thought and practice. "It is through first-hand experience of people and things that the child gains his first impressions and the channels for these impressions are his senses. 'Sense-training' has been a popular term in recent years in educational circles, but the idea that children learn through their senses, and only gradually come to be able to learn through words and symbols, has been the basis of much of the work of past educators of young children."[43] Fourier's contribution does not lie in the development of a psychology of sense training and perception. He merely adapted, albeit in a most exaggerated form, the theories of Condillac and Rousseau.[44] He was, however, aware of the importance of the senses and intuition in education, and sought to utilize them in his educational system. But in his work we do not find the details expected of a great practical educator such as Dr. Montessori or Margaret Macmillan.

Fourier's contribution is to bring out the wider possibilities for education of the senses within the everyday environment of the community. Comenius had written that "in order that everything may be imprinted the more easily on the mind, let the senses be applied to the subject as often as possible, e.g. let hearing be joined with vision, and the hand with speech".[45] Fourier perceived that this done in the 'normal' environment of the child might have important consequences. He maintains that with organization, the child will find pleasure, joy and satisfaction while working in the kitchens and gardens. And he does emphasize that these activities must be based upon the child's needs and desires and that they ought to be in accord with his abilities and aptitudes.

Gardening, cooking, dancing, singing, instrumental music making are all activities increasingly common in the school curriculum. Today we find educators insisting upon dramatic activities, ballet and 'modern' dancing. Moreover, there is an increasing tendency to emphasize dancing and acting which allow freedom of expression, free movement, and improvisation. Likewise, the need to educate in a more realistic environment and at a much earlier age is a theme much in the forefront of educational thought. Fourier was among the first to plead for these 'new methods' of education. His claim for 'cooking' and 'opera' was certainly exaggerated, but by overstating his case he drew attention to the immense possibilities of 'activity methods' in education long before the term had become commonplace in educational jargon.

1. S. Freud also wrote that "the little human being is frequently a finished product in his fourth or fifth year, and only gradually reveals in later years

what lies buried in him". *Introductory Lectures on Psycho-analysis* (1922), 298, quoted by H. Read, *Education for Free Men* (1944), 19.

2. *English Economic History*: *Select documents* edited by Brown, Bland and Tawney (1933), 502–3. In a few exceptional cases they might find work as early as three, again in the words of Owen: "Mr. Turner, treasurer to the Sunday School, knows a boy that was employed in a mill at Stockport when he was only three years old."

3. A. Léon, *Histoire de l'Education Technique* (1961), 57.
4. U. U., iv, 72–73.
5. U. U., iv, 75.
6. U. U., iv, 76.
7. U. U., iv, 74.
8. *Osnovy kommunisticheskogo vospitaniya*. Official joint publication of the Academy of Pedagogical Sciences and the Communist Party, Moscow (1962), 112–3.
9. U. U., iv, 105. "La gourmandise, divinité de tous les enfants."
10. U. U., iv, 104.
11. U. U., iv, 105–6.
12. U. U., iv, 110–111.
13. U. U., iv, 111.
14. U. U., iv, 102.
15. The epicures ("les spicius") are congenial companions well versed and absorbed in their art. They have, Fourier says, little in common with civilized children.
16. U. U., iv, 103.
17. U. U., iv, 95.
18. U. U., iv, 96.
19. U. U., iv, 96.
20. U. U., iv, 87–8.
21. U. U., iv, 89.
22. U. U., iv, 91.
23. Cp. Chapter 4.
24. The Jesuits at the Collège de Besançon had in fact encouraged theatrical representations. The importance of the theatre in the school curriculum was not neglected in the eighteenth century. See Louis Borne, *L'instruction Populaire en Franche-Comté avant 1792* (1949), ii, 417–37.
25. U. U., iv, 79.
26. U. U., iv, 82.
27. U. U., iv, 82.
28. U. U., iv, 82.
29. U. U., iv, 154.
30. U. U., iv, 77.
31. See next chapter.
32. U. U., iv, 77.
33. Cp. N. M., 223; U. U., iv, 77.
34. U. U., iv, 81.
35. I.e. over half of the members of the phalange.
36. U. U., iv, 81.

37. U. U., iv, 81.
38. U. U., iv, 81.
39. Recent research has shown more precisely how the type of language used handicaps the social and intellectual development of children. See *Education, Economy and Society* edited by A. H. Halsey (1961), Part IV, especially B. Bernstein's article "Social Class and Linguistic Development: A Theory of Social Learning", 288–314.
40. Mannheim and Stewart, *An Introduction to the Sociology of Education* (1962), 21.
41. U. U., iv, 82.
42. U. U., iv, 93.
43. E. Mellor, *Education through Experience* (1950), 13.
44. But unlike Rousseau he neglected the sense of touch.
45. Ibid., 13, quoted from S. S. Laurie, *John Amos Comenius*, 125.

CHAPTER SEVEN

The Teenage Period: a Time for Social Service

THE 'TEENAGE' period is recognized by Fourier as a time of difficulty and disturbance for the growing child. The development of impulses, peculiar to adolescence, the onset of puberty, the desire to serve and receive recognition from the community and yet remain in independent rebellion against it, the contradictory and persistent demands made by parents, teachers, friends and society, all these inevitably conflicting demands, says Fourier, create acute problems of adjustment for the child. These difficulties arise not only through conflicting demands, but also through the repression and diversion of the impulses of the child into unnatural channels.

Fourier's basic argument is that it is possible to develop moral qualities by social service to the community—channelling aggressive instincts and fondness for adornment to useful purposes.

In the first ten years, Fourier's educational provisions were designed to develop physical vigour, manipulative dexterity and love for industrial activity. In the next ten years, the psychological nature of the child's impulses is such that the development of moral values must dominate the education of the child and prevail over physical necessities.[1] It is a period of selfless devotion to the group. The dominant 'affective' passions of the child and adolescent from 9 to around 15 are, says Fourier, those of honour and friendship: his loyalty to his peer group overshadows that to his family, and sex feelings are as yet dormant.[2] It is thus a period, says Fourier, where pure disinterested friendship and selfless service are found. So it is during these years of adolescence that the impetus and desire for great and noble actions are at their greatest; and the opportunity must be found to enable the child to express them.

The child under nine is satisfied to develop his own skills, and rejoices in his new-found powers, good health and growing physical ability and dexterity. The time has now arrived to develop the soul and spirit, to give moral direction to the healthy and vigorous child. It is insufficient for the child to attain perfect health and wide technical competence: it is equally necessary that he learn to utilize his powers in socially virtuous production and useful study. The individual if he is to attain perfect harmony needs to give service to the community; so, argues Fourier, a Harmonious society demands and freely receives devoted and disinterested service. This duality is essential if the system is to function happily and efficiently.

Fourier believes that it is possible to organize a system which while allowing the adolescent full and unrestricted expression for his natural impulses also enables the adolescent to devote himself to the true interests of the community. He proposes means for turning anti-social behaviour into a valuable contribution to mankind, winning recognition, honours and privileges from adults, and hero worship and emulation from children.

Fourier suggests the founding of two independent children's societies, 'Les Petites Hordes' and 'Les Petites Bandes'. These two corporations of children aged 9 to $15\frac{1}{2}$ will be entirely voluntary, but Fourier rather optimistically asserts that all children in that age group will want to join one or other society. The Little Hordes will consist of those children with ardent, forceful and rebellious natures, inclined towards dirt and filth. Types who love to wallow in vileness and make it a mania playfully to indulge in indecency, who are peevish, roguish, obscene, who are arrogant and coarse, who are stimulated by noise and danger, who love destruction: all children with any or all of these impulses will find ample scope with the Little Hordes.

Children, on the other hand, who love tidiness, quiet, study, cleanliness will find a place among the Little Bands. Any child, irrespective of sex, may join the corporation of his choice: a boy with a taste for good manners and peaceful occupations would join the Little Band; while a girl with a boyish sense of fun, with an inclination to mannish behaviour, a tomboy, would enrol with the Little Hordes. The division between the two corporations will conform with the four cardinal temperaments: the bilious, sanguine, melancholy, and phlegmatic.[3] Individual temperaments will not necessarily be composed of one characteristic, but may be mixed. Fourier claims that the physiologists had ignored mixed temperaments, but he does not develop this point.

He does allow for a bilious-sanguine or a melancholy-phlegmatic character in the distribution of tasks among the two corporations. The possibility of alternative combinations, say a sanguine-phlegmatic, or a bilious-melancholy, character is not considered. This is perhaps because geometrically Fourier thought of the four temperaments as corresponding to points on a straight line, with bilious and phlegmatic characters on opposite extremes of the origin. Alternative combinations would have suggested themselves if he had represented his four cardinal temperaments as points along two perpendicular lines: in fact, utilizing Descartes's mathematical discovery. It is interesting to note that this later graphical method is now a common technique in the study of human personality.[4]

Fourier's division of children into the rowdy and phlegmatic is obviously open to the charge that it is exceedingly simple. It may perhaps be answered that it is no more so than our own English division of children into 'grammar' and 'secondary modern'. Fourier estimated that the Little Hordes will enrol approximately twice as many boys as girls, while within the Little Bands girls will outnumber boys in the same ratio.[5] Each of the two corporations will be divided into three groups with the aim of giving a wider choice of activity to the varying gradations of temperaments.

The Little Hordes are divided into three groups: the first performs the dirty tasks of the community such as the cleaning of sinks, sewers, privies, the management of manures, etc.; the second specializes in the more skilled menial tasks, e.g. the destruction of reptiles and insects, roadmending, etc.; the third is an auxiliary group which participates in the functions of both.[6]

In the society called 'civilized', says Fourier, the aggressive children become restless, dissatisfied, bored. They tend to form gangs, to go about getting dirty, destroying property, causing general mischief. For example, in the absence of constructive entertainment, they might spend the evening smearing the knockers and bell-handles of a neighbourhood with dirt. These pranks, asserts Fourier, give them immense pleasure, and they delight in playing them upon everybody. Their plots, he says, are well planned and dexterously executed; and even when the children are occasionally caught and beaten, their 'noble ardour' remains untarnished.[7]

Fourier's aim and purpose are to sublimate the aggressive instincts of childhood (which he clearly recognized) into socially desirable channels.[8] He has a solution for what might be called the problems of the 'Teddy-boys', the 'Stilyagi' and the 'Zoot-suiters'. The Little Hordes must inevitably be barbarous in their activities and in their dress, but in his scheme this barbarism need not produce anti-social behaviour.[9] In the world as it is, youngsters rebel against the inadequate opportunities and the unnatural restrictions for self-expression, they adopt an aggressive and destructive attitude towards society out of a sense of emotional frustration; whereas in Fourier's Harmony, although the energies of all are given full scope, teenage aggression harms no one, for the youthful energies are positively channelled into socially challenging and useful pursuits. The organization of the Little Hordes encourages the natural exclusiveness of children and teenagers but it endeavours to utilize the social cohesion of the age group as an asset. Everything is done to make the Little Hordes feel a cohesive group: they have their own language or jargon; their own artillery (to kill reptiles); their own generals (or gang-leaders), whom Fourier entitles the 'Petits Kans' and 'Petites Kantes'[10] They each have a private vocabulary and adopt grotesque nicknames.[11]

Although the Little Hordes will be an autonomous corporation, there will still be the need for adults to assist and direct the Argot in its work.[12] These adults will be chosen from among those who have preserved their taste for repugnant and dirty work: who have not outgrown the pleasures of adolescence. These aides ('acolytes') will bear the title of "Druides et Druidesses de l'Argot", or "Coëres et Coëresses—titre que les mendiants civilisés donnent à leur président ou chef des gueux".[13] They will also need to have participated in a dozen campaigns in the industrial armies[14] before assuming their titles.

Fourier says that it was precisely because he at first failed to see the importance of this 'mania for dirt' that some crucial problems of his system remained unsolved. In endeavouring, at first, to have this peculiarity of children disappear, Fourier was acting, as he put it, like a Titan who wished to change the work of God.[15] It was not until he adopted a different attitude and sought to utilize the inclinations of children, as nature created them, that success came his way. The taste for dirt is a necessary impulse to enlist children in the corporation of the Little Hordes, to induce them to undergo daily the inconveniences connected with dirty work. The Freudians have also stressed the association of dirt with pleasure. They point to such phrases as 'stinking with money', 'filthy lucre', 'throwing money down the drain', and even 'rolling in the stuff', which all equate money with faeces. They ask why the concern over punctuality and cleanliness is sometimes carried to pathological degrees if it is not to be regarded as a reaction against a primitive wish for dirt and disorder.[16] Fourier does not analyse this 'mania'; he merely observes its prevalence and its force, and he seeks to utilize it. And in so doing, he says, he at the same time solved the problem of the execution of repugnant and filthy work. Work which degrades the self-esteem of the individual, and is consequently performed by the dregs of society, will in his utopia be undertaken on a collective basis by the Little Hordes as an act of social charity. Thus, in addition to providing an indispensable service to the community, the Little Hordes provide training in moral and social responsibilities: and open for themselves, "dans la carrière de la cochonnerie, un vaste champ de gloire industrielle et de philanthropie unitaire".[17]

Fourier argues vigorously against payment for repugnant work. In complete Harmony, not a penny will be appropriated to the payment of unclean work.[18] He does not believe that even large sums would compensate for the indignity and social ostracism associated with workers in disgusting occupations.

This opinion is rejected by two contemporary American sociologists, Robert S. Weiss and David Riesman, who comment thus on the above suggestion by "the brilliant and erratic utopian theorist" Charles Fourier: "Our national reaction against child labor, and our commitment, as a nation, to the view that childhood is to be reserved for social and intellectual development, will prevent this notion from being taken seriously by us (unless we can urge that some work develops 'character'). A more acceptable idea than Fourier's is that by increasing the pay and lowering the hours of the most disagreeable jobs people might be recruited who wouldn't mind holding them, at least for a time".[19] Fourier would answer that they miss his point. He believes that distasteful tasks would not normally attract sufficient people of skill and wealth; only those endowed with no special talent would participate for financial reward, but the rich and the more intelligent would desist from joining. This would merely create barriers of class similar to those in present society where the disgust felt for dirt, and the menial tasks associated with it, divide those engaged in it from the rest of society. This attitude has repercussions in the education of children in that it creates in parents a hysterical desire to keep their children clean and a powerful ambition never to see them in the menial occupations. It is essential for the harmonious functioning of society that there be no single kind of labour which is despised, considered ignoble and degrading for the class that engages in it. For instance, if there were boot-blacks in Harmony, those children, and consequently their parents, would be counted an inferior class.[20] The debasement would spread from one sort of labour to another, the contempt for labour would be gradually revived, and the result will be that those people would be termed 'comme il faut' who do nothing and are good for nothing. Then the time would come when this wealthy class would no longer take any part in industry and agriculture and would disdain to have any social relations with the poor.[21]

Fourier is highly critical of acts of useless and pretentious charity: examples he cites are the washing of the feet of the poor by sovereigns on Holy Thursday, which in any case, he says, they could very well do themselves; or employing a confessor with an income of 50,000 francs to detach a criminal from the gallows. Civilized charitable practices are ineffectual. They have, for him, no economic merit. They do nothing to draw together the upper and lower classes essentially because they fail to raise the lower orders from their undignified and unpleasant state.[22] The Little Hordes will undertake all distasteful work, and thus preserve the social order from the evils of class conflict. They will always be up and about at three o'clock in the morning (they go to bed at eight) cleaning the stables, attending to the animals, working in the slaughter houses, where they are on the watch to see that no unnecessary suffering is ever inflicted upon the animals put to death.[23] Later, they will also do the dirty work in the kitchens, the infirmaries,[24] the roads, sewers, privies, and any other unpleasant work held in disdain. Thus children labouring for the mass and not for an individual, will practise corporatively the only branch of charity remaining in Harmony. This will be so since, once the poor have disappeared and wealth abounds, there will be no other form of service to the community left for children to take up except in the domain of unclean labour; and this the Little Hordes will do on a collective basis.

Ideas strikingly similar to these have been put forward by Dr. M. F. Yates in a lecture to the English New Education Fellowship in London.[25] Though she was not reported as mentioning Fourier by name, she said that, "All young people, both boys and girls, should do a year of service to the community. In these days of 'the fag-end of Empire' young people were bored, she said, and needed to find a dynamic".

"They would find it, she thought, by spending a year doing the 'bedrock tasks' in the community. They could become dustbin collectors, porters, hospital orderlies, they could work in kitchens and canteens—doing anything, in fact, that required no special qualifications. Young people were anxious to do good these days and they would enjoy the experience.

"They would all, of course, be paid a basic rate, whatever they were doing. The scheme would help to remove the distinction between children from state and independent schools. It would be democratic and would give a boost to the welfare state.

"Dr. Yates said that she was prepared to contemplate legislation making this year's service compulsory.

"Her point of reference for this project was the Voluntary Service Overseas scheme. She had met boys who had come back from doing this and had found that though they had originally intended to go into banking or some such career, they were now determined to devote themselves to social service. This enthusiasm could be kindled in this country. It could be the cure of the 'age of the shrug'."

The Editor of the *Times Educational Supplement* in a leading article commented: "Dr. M. F. Yates makes a valuable point in suggesting that all young people should do a period of social service. She is less happy in her ideas about the form it should take . . . They should have to take on the 'bedrock tasks' of the community, the tasks, that is, that require no special qualifications. Now the point about Voluntary Service Overseas, which she uses as an analogy for her scheme, is not only that boys go out to exotic parts of the world but that once there they have very considerable responsibility. They find themselves up against difficulties that call forth every ounce of ability they have. This is very rewarding, but quite different from what Dr. Yates proposes. Collecting dustbins is a very valuable and necessary activity, but it is no challenge. The point, however, should not be lost; a national scheme of social service could be valuable both to the individual and to society."

It is even more interesting to note that some eighteen months later the same journal reported an experiment in community service in Britain that had been under way for a year and a half.[26] This new venture had in fact been started by the founder of Voluntary Service Overseas, Mr. Alec Dickson. Mr. Dickson's ideas for the establishment of a home voluntary service arose out of his experience abroad. His now established Community of Service Volunteers caters for young people, aged 18 to 21, who work among young offenders in remand homes, approved schools, borstals and detention centres; among the sick and disabled in general hospitals, Cheshire homes and mental institutions, among children in care at reception centres, orphanages and homes; among the aged in geriatric wards and old people's homes. Fourier envisaged involving young people in so-called 'dirty' and 'degrading' work of the community. He argued that self-sacrifice and selfless service was worth while, not only to the individual, but also to the community. These ideas are as relevant then as now: Dr. Yates' lecture and Mr. Dickson's work are but two interesting and important illustrations.[27]

Fourier, perhaps too naïvely, assumes that children will thus produce and maintain general friendship among all classes, which has been so long the dream of politicians and philosophers. If in Association, the people are refined, upright, and above want, there can exist no distrust or contempt on the part of the rich towards the poorer classes. A friendly enthusiasm therefore will be aroused in all industrial groups, where the masses mingle with the great. Thus the dream of making mankind a family of brothers will also be realized.[28]

The régime of attraction would fail utterly, unless it succeeded in attaching powerful baits to repellent kinds of labour: in an order of things in which pleasure is the prime mover in the social mechanism, repugnance must be overcome by attraction.[29] The Little Hordes in undertaking the most unpleasant and repugnant work of the phalange will be attracted to it by self-respect, friendship and devotion to the community.[30] The inclination for dirt, compulsive though it is, does not in itself provide sufficient incentive. The love of dirt in children is like a wild fruit, as yet an uncultivated germ. It is merely the starting basis for the development of moral sentiments. The child needs allurements before its taste for filthy activity is channelled into socially useful and constructive purposes. Indirect methods of attraction are imperative; repugnant occupations must be turned into enjoyable and satisfying games.[31] The essential need is to refine the inclination for dirt, and this can best be done by applying to it two forces or impulses—*the unitary religious spirit* and *corporative honour*.[32]

Though Fourier is a critic of almost every aspect of the education of his time, his system for the Argot has the same psychological basis as regards motivation. As Durkheim has pointed out[33] the motivational basis of medieval Christian education was the idea of duty, which the Renaissance replaced by that of honour, reward and personal glory. Fourier makes a slight modification of this. He introduces collective responsibility and loyalty to the group. He endeavours to make the group cohesive, he emphasizes its separatedness, so attempts to create an accepted code of behaviour—a code, which he is aware, so successfully operates among brigands and robbers. There is 'honour among thieves', and the honour with which criminals adhere to their code, even under threat of dire consequence, indicates that social expectation has passed into genuine personal acceptance. Fourier shows considerable insight in endeavouring to use social approval and ostracism to create in each individual a sense of socially accepted dignity or socially expected conduct.

H

It is interesting to note that honour plays a similar part not only in primitive society[34] but also in our advanced industrial society.

Fourier is aware that repugnant work is unpleasant, uninteresting, repetitive, hardly likely to appeal to the imagination, or to be rewarding in itself. Hence he argues that there is a great need for strong emotive allurements. He believes that the religious spirit (he cites the example of the Redemptionist fathers) engenders a devotion to general charity, and he utilizes this inclination in his schemes. An emotive quasi-religious crusading atmosphere is thus generated in the activities of the Little Hordes in the endeavour to invoke a devotion to abject work. Fourier outlines with obvious relish his ideas for the elaborate ceremonies which will precede and terminate the brief sessions actually devoted to the unpleasant work.[35] These ceremonies, as well as enthusing the participants, are designed to emphasize the useful social and religious nature of the work of the Little Hordes.

The simple and direct repugnance of the work involved in the management of the sewers and the cleaning of the privies, one of the more important responsibilities of the Little Hordes, need most to be counterbalanced, "par amorce composée indirecte".[36] The shortness of all sessions, here as in all other series, is the first of these baits: no sessions need exceed 1½ hours. The work will be organized to give the impression of a massive feast. The social nature and importance of the occasion will be emphasized by the presence of several neighbouring "cohortes": all will assemble for a "repas matinal" at 4.45 a.m. Afterwards in the company of other groups who begin their work at 5 a.m., they will parade and sing a religious hymn. The Little Hordes then, to the accompaniment of "un tintamarre de tocsin, carillons, tambours, trompettes, hurlements de dogues et mugissements de boeufs", will, led by their leaders, the Kans and Druides, pass in review before the Patriarches "qui les aspergent". They will then hasten fervently to work, which they will carry out as an act of piety, an act of charity towards the phalange ("service de Dieu et de l'unité").[37] The work done, they will wash themselves and disperse into the various gardens and workshops until 8 a.m. when they will breakfast together. During the meal each of the Hordes will receive a cluster of oak or pine, to be attached to their flag. After breakfast the visitors will return to their respective phalange.

The roads in Harmony are considered "comme salon de l'unité", and the Little Hordes "à titre de charité unitaire" are responsible for their condition. They will keep these in beautiful order: their borders will be ornamented with trees and shrubberies, and even flowers. Immediately damage is discovered on any of the roads, the alarm will be given, be this even in the middle of the night, the appropriate section of the Argot (the 'sacripants') will set off at once (equipped with suitable torches if necessary) to repair the damage, and hoist an accident signal over the place, for fear that the damage may not be noticed by some travellers, who may be injured, and so give rise to an accusation against the phalange of having bad 'sacripants'. It would likewise be accused of having bad 'chenopants', if a vicious reptile, serpent or viper were discovered, or a croaking of frogs be heard anywhere near the highroads.[38] These activities are not dissimilar to those of the social service units at Gordonstoun, where the boys man a fire-station and help the coast-guards.

The care, treatment, and prevention of cruelty to animals will be another primary responsibility of the Argot.[39] Domestic animals, birds, fish and insects must all be well looked after and well treated. Offenders who fail in this respect, or cause unnecessary suffering in the slaughter houses, will be apprehended by the Argot, and if necessary indicted before a tribunal of children, "comme inférieur en raison aux enfants mêmes" and even stupider than the animals themselves.

Fourier's concern for animals and his plea for their kind treatment was derived from his own love for them; he was especially fond of cats. He argued that they had souls, that they were useful and that care would enhance their utility.[40] Rousseau and Condorcet also urged kindness to animals and the manuals of moral education prescribed for French children during the Third Republic finally brought this doctrine into the schools. Nevertheless, the destruction of malicious reptiles, serpents and vipers will be necessary. This dangerous task, naturally to the accompaniment of much prescribed ceremony, will be undertaken, as we have seen, by the 'chenopans'.[41]

Although, in default of direct attraction, the work of the Argot is difficult and unpleasant, they will remain the least remunerated series. They will always accept the very smallest reward: they will scorn and despise 'indirect' riches. Moreover, their finest prerogative will be their ability to give away one eighth of their family fortune to the phalange and in making this sacrifice they will be serving God's purpose—"puisque la cause de l'unité est celle de Dieu".[42] Thus in the interest of the happiness of society, they will practise "l'abnégation de soi-même" recommended by Christianity, and "le mépris des richesses" recommended by philosophy.[43]

Assuredly, says Fourier, it is most objectionable to accord a child of nine the right to dispose of a portion of his inheritance. This permission could indeed in civilization lead to dangerous and shocking abuses. Not so in Harmony, where the money is distributed by the Argot at the annual accounting meeting of the phalange in full view of all the inhabitants. This renunciation of the inherited means will be a wonderful and practical method of maintaining the cardinal virtue—that of industrial honour (so vital to the esprit de corps of the Little Hordes and the entire phalange).[44]

It is conceivable that several series may make a loss over the year, and so at the annual accounting meeting will find themselves at a monetary disadvantage. Here will be an opportunity for the Little Hordes to make up the deficit and enable the defaulting series to start the new financial year with all its debts paid. The 'Petit Kan' (the chief of the Horde) will hand over the money to the defaulting series amid much ceremony and before the fully assembled phalange. This loss of face, for the defaulting series, will encourage its members to work harder and more efficiently and so avoid public shame. The self-sacrifice of the hardest worked and least remunerated of the series, l'Argot, their disinterested and generous donations to those unable to fully meet their obligations, will be a source of immense encouragement and a shining example to the rest of the phalange.[45]

The Little Hordes will also occupy a prominent place in the ranks of the industrial armies. Theirs will be the privilege of first partaking in new campaigns.[46] Association, in sharp contrast to civilization, will assemble productive armies instead of destructive ones. Civilization enlists its heroes by compulsion, the Harmonians will be attracted to the industrial armies by the allurement of 'fêtes' and pleasures unknown to civilization, where an army of a hundred thousand men knows no other collective pleasure but that of destroying, burning, pillaging, and ravishing. In spite of the jeremiads upon the penurious condition of the finances every state does in fact raise immense sums for the provision of these destructive bodies. Fourier says that he heard a Russian engineer tell of how, at the siege of Rustchuk, in 1811, every bomb thrown into that city cost Russia 400 francs in transportation costs alone! "Que de dépenses pour la destruction des hommes et des édifices!" he laments. What a fortunate change it would be for a society which could assemble such bodies for useful and constructive purposes. How is it, he goes on to ask, that our constructors of utopias ("nos faiseurs d'utopies") have not dared to dream of "une réunion de 500,000 hommes occupés à construire au lieu de détruire!"[47] The expenditure, he points out with the logic of a commercial traveller, would be much smaller for a productive army; and besides the saving in slaughtered men, burnt cities, devastated fields, we should have the saving of the cost of equipment, and the benefit of the work accomplished.[48]

The failure of society to produce and even sustain any great projects, Fourier attributes to its inability to raise industrial armies. The Pyramids and Lake Moeris are no trophies of civilization but monuments of oppression of man. These were built by employing hosts of slaves driven by the whip and by torture. The work of the Harmonians will be vastly superior to that which could possibly be accomplished by a body of slaves and wage-earners, all agreed in shirking labour. The Harmonians, with the Argot in the vanguard, for whom the work is transformed into a 'fete' and a matter of pride, will be so much the more successful.[49] The mere thought of the work which the industrial armies would attempt, claimed Fourier, would freeze the civilized mercenary soul with horror. The Harmonians would, for example, reclaim the great desert of the Sahara: transporting earth, cultivating the soil, planting trees, five, or if necessary ten, million people helping to make the region fruitful. Canals, for irrigation and transport, would also be constructed there and elsewhere throughout the world. Great ships will be able to sail not only across isthmuses like those of Suez and Panama, but even in the interior of continents, as from the Caspian Sea to the Sea of Azov, as from Quebec to the five great lakes; finally, it will be possible to navigate from the sea to all the great lakes whose lengths equal a quarter of their distance to the sea.[50]

Had Fourier been still alive to-day, how much pleasure he would have derived from writing to the statesmen of the world urging them to raise industrial armies, and to utilize the youth of the world in constructive endeavours. Instead of using the Sahara to test nuclear bombs with which to blow ourselves up, how much better to turn the area into a fertile plain. It is not inconceivable, particularly during a World Freedom from Hunger campaign, of peaceful armies being recruited to cultivate the Sahara. The U.S. Peace Corps and Britain's V.S.O. organizations are not dissimilar in aim from what Fourier first envisaged.

In contrast to the difficult and unpleasant tasks of the Little Hordes, the diametrically opposed functions of the Little Bands are most "attractive" and "easy". In his *Unité Universelle*, Fourier confines himself to defining their tasks and leaves the choice of names "aux amateurs du romantique",[51] but only to take up his own challenge in 1826.[52] He divides the Little Bands into three groups: the first group, for the cultivation of good manners, general adornment and the fine arts, he names "les Troubadours"; the second, for study, easy work ("les études et travaux faciles et le luxe d'agriculture"), he names "les Ménestrels"; thirdly are "les Prosélytes", who will not confine themselves to either but will participate in both.

The maintenance of passionate equilibrium necessitates that the functions of "la Chevalerie" (the corporation of the Little Bands) will be diametrically opposed to those of the Argot. For the more active the Little Hordes become and the greater their devotion to social service, the more acute becomes the need for a rival corporation. This gives rise, says Fourier, to an interesting problem in "moral equilibrium"[53] for the Little Bands: how to counterbalance the fervency of their rivals; what means must be utilized if they are to attain a degree of religious zeal which can rival that displayed by the Argot. The solution, for Fourier, is to cultivate the dominant taste of girls, because they are in the majority within the Little Bands "et ce goût est évidemment celui de LA PARURE". Effeminate boys will also belong to the Little Bands, and 'soft' ones with inclinations for a sybaritic or voluptuous life, as well as clever young boys with precocious minds—"like Pascal's"—who early display a vocation for learning.

The rivalry of the two corporations, says Fourier, is sufficient to create within the Little Bands a tone and manners diametrically opposite to those of the Argot. The differences in manners between the two is as pronounced as the disparity between soldiers and lawyers. The Little Bands will be extremely polite. Their dominant taste is for "atticisme", or refinement. They will display manners equal to those seen in the best circles of Paris and London; and in addition a great desire to excel in the sciences and arts.[54] Whereas the Little Hordes conspicuously overcome material obstacles, the Little Bands must excel in attaining spiritual supremacy. The Little Bands are generally more industrious, except of course, that the Little Hordes are specialists in horsemanship, the care of horses, ponies and dogs, hunting and fishing. However, the Little Bands do look after animals requiring tender and patient care such as zebras, beavers, bees, etc.[55] The enthusiasm of the Little Hordes will also be doubled in intensity by the indirect competition from their natural rivals. Thus they will mutually complement and benefit each other.

The critic in civilization, Fourier surmises, may well argue that this taste for adornment on which so much depends is really a source of evil influence and most unlikely to provide the basis for developing a counterbalance to the social work of the Little Hordes. This will indeed be so, if the taste for adornment is misdirected and misapplied; and, as if to terminate the argument, he quotes in support of his thesis the common proverb: "Jamais mauvais ouvrier n'a su trouver bon outil." The taste for frivolity, for baubles, he asserts, so foolishly wasted in civilization on dolls, will in Harmony create a second palladium of social happiness,[56] provided it is utilized collectively and never individually.

The activities of the Chivalry, hardly less valuable than those of the Argot (although only meriting the rank of an important branch of industry) will, says Fourier, produce four wonders:

the refinement of industry, the domination of good taste, compound instruction, compound friendship. These will give rise to social charm within the phalange, create a feeling of ardent enthusiasm for its institutions and its work, and affection for all its visitors.[57]

The Little Bands are responsible for the care, protection and surveillance of the domain of plants.[58] Fourier, always a lover of flowers, sees to it that they will be well cared for in Harmony. He would have the Little Bands pay special attention to flowers. Flowers, he says, are a source of charm and refinement; and he believes that growing and looking after flowers develops these very attitudes in the gardener. Moreover, he considers it a gross error to maintain that, apart from their aesthetic value, flowers are useless. The passion for flowers, in fact, says Fourier, is designed by nature to draw the female sex to horticulture. Once the bases have been firmly established the child will desire to extend her experience beyond the flower bed, to the orchard, the kitchen garden, the greenhouse.[59] To attain this end, therefore, the cultivation and care of the flowers are of special value and occupy a high place among the activities of the Little Bands. Each phalange will establish an academy "*de jeux floraux composés*. Il ne sont que *simples* à Toulouse, où on récompense la culture des fleurs de l'esprit". He gives no further details about this proposed academy.[60]

The Little Bands will develop the same attitudes towards their flower beds as the Little Hordes for the roads. They will be growers as well as florists, with the responsibility of exhibiting these in various public meeting places within the phalange. They will accept responsibility for the entire phalange. Anyone found breaking branches of trees, picking flowers or fruit without need, negligently treading on plants, will be indicted before the Senate of the Chivalry, where judgement will be passed in accord with the penal code then in force!

The Little Bands will exercise the functions of the "académie française et della Crusca".[61] They will censure bad language and vicious pronunciation. Not only the language of their contemporaries but also that of their fathers will be included within this purview. Their Senate will have the right to catalogue any pronunciation and grammatical mistakes made by adults. Frequent offenders will find themselves recipients of a list of their errors, duly certified by the president and chancellor of the Senate, with an invitation to reform.

This privilege and right of literary criticism is bestowed upon the Little Bands with the idea that it will encourage them to study. They will be unable to detect errors of speech unless they themselves are aware of the accepted forms. This opportunity for study will, so Fourier believes, attract studious children to the Chivalry. The double stimulant to study—the right of criticism and corporate pretensions—will create an atmosphere of literary lustre and good taste among the corporation and give birth to pride and self-respect within the corporation.

These corporative activities of the Little Bands, Fourier seems to think, will prove so influential that in their turn they will spread pride in speech and manners, good taste, and self-respect among the masses, so generating "l'Amitié composée".[62] Fourier makes the point that, since as he believes ostentatious egotism is the dominant motive in simple or individual friendship, this type of personal relationship is vain, anti-social and altogether undesirable. He seems to anticipate the distinction between 'friend' and 'comrade'.[63] He wishes to encourage only collective and socially orientated relationships. And so, stimulated, as Fourier hopes they will be, by the spectacular, but virtuous and charitable examples of the Little Hordes, the Little Bands will concern themselves solely with their collective adornment and the general lustre of the phalange. Those suspected of egotism and "l'esprit civilisé" will be despised.[64]

The Chivalry has responsibilities for the initiation of all elegant, agreeable and ornamental works. The Little Bands are thus always the first to begin new projects associated with work requiring, not brute force, but rather skill and ingenuity: miniature arts and crafts, literary activity connected with the opera, the temple and the altar.[65]

Although the two corporations go to bed at about the same time, they get up at different times. The Little Bands rise later than the others and do not begin work before 4 a.m. There is no need for them to do otherwise, for they are not responsible for any of the larger animals, with the notable exception of their zebras. Instead they look after animals difficult to rear, e.g. carrier pigeons, bees, etc., who need no early morning sessions as do those who come under the care of the Argot.[66]

All are entirely free in Harmony to wear what they will; but while meeting as a corporation uniforms are necessary.[67] The Little Bands will wear cavalier and romantic clothes, adapted from either ancient or modern times. The Little Bands in each phalange will have clothes radically different from those worn in the neighbouring phalange. Thus if those living in Saint-Cloud adopt Troubadourian dress, the Marly crowd will sally forth in Athenian dress. This is in marked contrast to the uniforms of the Little Hordes which are of the same pattern for all in each province, though each in a different colour "de sorte que chaque horde en manoeuvre espacée a l'éclat d'un carreau de tulipes toutes différenciés de leurs voisines".[68]

Until such time as it becomes possible to provide the Little Bands with zebras and mount their attendants, the "corybants et corybantes" on quaggas, both will use ponies.[69] Their rectilinear manoeuvres will be in sharp contrast to the curvilinear display of the Little Hordes. Fourier gives details of the differences and compares them with those used by the cossacks. He explains that though this may seem to be of little interest, they are mentioned to illustrate the differences between the two corps and the need for these exercises in the enhancement of the cabalistic spirit.[70]

The Little Bands are not permitted by the "Aréopage"[71] to dispose of one-eighth of their inheritance. Instead they may give away such saving as they may have accumulated, while still bambins, cherubins and seraphins, to defray the expenses of collective luxury. They may not utilize them for individual adornment. The utilization of these savings is permitted "parce que c'est semer pour recueillir".[72]

This devotion to beautiful things at first encouraged by what may seem frivolous and inconsequential attractions, such as flowers and clothes, will in time grow to include the fine arts, and later the sciences and industry. The effect of his system is such, Fourier insists, that all work becomes closely linked: one branch leading to another. It is therefore immaterial that a section of the child population should devote themselves to what may be at first considered frivolous—they will, Fourier is convinced, eventually proceed to the useful. It will become recognized that this taste for adornment, so harmful and obnoxious in civilization, will become the basis of industrial progress when exercised *collectively*.[73] Thus he hopes that here among the Little Bands his system will give birth to 'good things' utilizing the taste for 'beautiful things'; whereas the Little Hordes utilize 'good things' to give birth to 'beautiful things'.[74]

These are all educational activities which naturally suggest themselves, says Fourier, in any study of the nature of boys and girls. Lack of knowledge of the nature of the child, ignorance of the impulses and of the peculiarities of the different sexes, have all made study and learning much harder for the child than it need be. The neglect of the principle of composite adornment has in particular led to the inability of the civilized to give girls an education suitable and in accord with their need and nature. Civilized education of girls is restrictive and narrow because it is based on the assumption that woman was made purely for the pleasure of the male, a view he attributes to the teaching of Mohammed and Rousseau.[75] Fourier is intent on extending opportunities for girls beyond the kitchen and the horizon of domestic chores. Women, he emphasizes, have distinct contributions of their own to make to society. These contributions, as Fourier claims to have shown in describing the activities of the Little Hordes and Bands, are complementary to the pursuits of the male. Rivalry between the sexes is indispensable for the development and continual efflorescence of their mutually complementary selves.

Fourier's ideas on adolescent education can thus be seen to have, like the rest of his work, a certain number of fantastic or fanciful elements, but also insights and suggestions which recur in modern educational thought. He is aware of the problem of freedom and free choice. He wishes to preserve the individuality of the adolescent, but he also recognizes the individual's need for creative recognized service to the community. The contribution of young people, their capacity and desire to be of service, has been persistently under-estimated and only very reluctantly allowed scope of expression. Fourier argued that the repression of the adolescent's willingness and enthusiasm can but lead to a feeling of rejection, separateness and futility. The inability of the adolescent to find a socially recognized purpose in our own time has led to a situation not dissimilar to that predicted by Fourier. In their "crisis of identity", in their endeavour to answer the question "Who am I?" adolescents need adult help (but not interference) otherwise, as Professor Carstairs has shown,[76] the "malaise of adolescents" becomes widespread. And so in his endeavours to find social recognition and significance, it is essential, as Fourier emphasized, and Professor Dobinson has more recently urged, "to give young people a chance to contribute to the welfare of the community as soon as they are ready for it".[77] It is interesting to see experiments in voluntary service not dissimilar to those advocated by Fourier now under way in Britain and overseas.[78] The importance of voluntary service for the health and happiness of the society, particularly of an Affluent Society, cannot be exaggerated, and Fourier deserves greater recognition than he has received as an early thinker on problems of adolescence and society.

1. U. U., iv, 131.
2. U. U., iv, 159. The development of these two other affective passions is discussed in the next chapter.
3. U. U., iv, 171.
4. See e.g. H. J. Eysenck, *The Scientific Study of Personality* (1952), 259, 273, 285.
5. N. M., 207.
6. U. U., iv, 144; see also Manus. (1852), 172. Fourier called the first group, the "Sacripans" or "Zélateurs"; the second, the "Chenopans" or "Hériques"; the third, the "Garnements" or "Coadjuteurs".
7. U. U., iv, 158.
8. It is interesting to find an influential member of the British school of psycho-analysts writing, "The repeated attempts that have been made to improve humanity—in particular to make it more peaceable—have failed, because nobody has understood the full depth and vigour of the instincts of aggression innate in each individual. Such efforts do not seek to do more than encourage the positive, well-wishing impulses of the person while denying or suppressing his aggressive ones. And so they have been doomed to failure from the beginning." See Melanie Klein, "The Early Development of Conscience in the Child", in *Psycho-Analysis Today* (edited by Sándor Lorand), London, 1948, 73.
9. U. U., iv, 144-5.
10. These titles are presumably derived from the Asian Khan.
11. Their language Fourier has named "l'Argot", and the various Horde officials are often referred to as ". . . de l'Argot".
12. For the position of the adult in Harmonian education see Chapter 4.
13. U. U., iv, 145.
14. See supra.
15. Ibid., 161.
16. Cp. J. A. C. Brown, *Freud and the Post-Freudians*, London (1962), 23.

17. U. U., iv, 159.
18. U. U., iii, 531.
19. See "Social Problems and Disorganization in the World of Work", 472, in a collection of essays entitled *Contemporary Social Problems*, edited by R. K. Merton and R. A. Nisbet, New York, 1961.
20. U. U., iv, 163. However, "it is rarely necessary to clean one's shoes in Harmony, thanks to the covered ways!"
21. U. U., iv, 160.
22. Cp. U. U., iv, 393-4.
23. U. U., iv, 163.
24. Except attending the sick, which, says Fourier, can only be entrusted to a body of mature persons. U. U., iv, 161.
25. *The Times Educational Supplement*, 23 February 1962.
26. 20 September 1963.
27. Some of the problems of growth in this area are discussed in the Bessey Report, *Service by Youth* (H.M.S.O.), 1966.
28. U. U., iv, 162, 163.
29. U. U., iv, 138.
30. Manus. (1852), 197.
31. "Jeux d'attraction INDIRECT COMPOSEE" (sic), U. U., lv, 159.
32. U. U., iv, 159.
33. Emile Durkheim, *L'Evolution Pédagogigue en France*, Vol. II, Paris (1938), *passim*.
34. See e.g., B. Malinowski, *Sex and Repression in Savage Society* (1927).
35. Cp. Manus. (1852), 200.
36. U. U., iv, 148.
37. U. U., iv, 142.
38. U. U., iv, 150.
39. U. U., iv, 155.
40. Cp. M. Ferraz, *Nos devoirs et nos droits* (1881), 356.
41. U. U., iv, 150.
42. U. U., iv, 150.
43. N. M., 209.
44. U. U., iv, 151. Another educational advantage, which Fourier seems to have overlooked, is that the children's participation at the annual accounting meeting will offer an excellent opportunity for the introduction of the principles of economics and administration.
45. Cp. U. U., iv, 140.
46. U. U., iv, 154.
47. U. U., iii, 561.
48. Cp. current controversy: "Cut defence expenditure to provide more teachers and school buildings."
49. U. U., iv, 562. Normally each army will comprise men, women and children, in the ratio 3 : 2 : 1 respectively.
50. Q. M., 263. Cp. ii, 97.
51. U. U., iv, 172.
52. See Manus. (1852), 172.
53. U. U., iv, 175.

54. U. U., iv, 168.
55. U. U., iv, 169.
56. U. U., iv, 175.
57. U. U., iv, 176.
58. U. U., iv, 155, 176, "les Petites Bandes ont la haute police du règne végétal".
59. U. U., iv, 176.
60. U. U., iv, 177.
61. U. U., iv, 178.
62. U. U., iv, 178.
63. Cp. 'friend' and 'comrade' in Soviet pedagogy. See M. Waddington's article in *Communist Education*, ed. E. J. King (1963), 72-3.
64. U. U., iv, 179.
65. U. U., iv, 180.
66. U. U., iv, 170.
67. N. M., 214.
68. U. U., iv, 169.
69. Aged acolytes corresponding to the "coëres et coëresses" of the hordes.
70. U. U., iv, 170.
71. "Ou Conseil suprême de direction du phalanstère . . . Il indique les travaux à exécuter mais ne les ordonne pas." U. U., iii, 447.
72. U. U., iv, 172.
73. U. U., iv, 170.
74. U. U., iv, 174. "Les Petites Hordes marchent au beau par la route du bon: Les Petites Bandes marchent au bon par la route du beau."
75. U. U., iv, 180.
76. In the third of his Reith Lectures, see *The Listener*, 29.11.1963.
77. C. H. Dobinson, *Schooling 1963-1970*, 156.
78. These ideas are spreading widely and at great speed. The work of the International Secretariat for Volunteer Service is evidence of the adoption of community service by the young on an international scale.

CHAPTER EIGHT

Growing Up:
the Problem of Sex and Education

FOURIER must be one of the earliest writers to give consideration to the place of sex in education. Once again his treatment of this question is a combination of great modernity and wild imagination. Fourier is aware of the difficulties that others will have in following his revelations and partly to allay their fears he invites them to imagine that he is describing the love life of adolescents of another planet.[1]

Fourier believed that men are by nature promiscuous[2] and that women are not intended for marriage.[3] Moreover, Fourier maintained that with the advent of an average future expectancy of one hundred and fifty years, marriage will become intolerable. His strong disapproval of marriage, his desire to abolish the family, his strong feminism,[4] his psychological stress on the importance of preventing emotional and sexual frustration, all combine to make freedom of sexual behaviour an indispensable tenet of his system. He advocates trial marriage and free love.

These extreme views, apart from throwing discredit on his opinions as a whole, have naturally given considerable offence to many, brought him much criticism,[5] and caused him not a little embarrassment: for no subject then as now, as the Secretary of the Marriage Guidance Council has remarked, "makes some people more disturbed and indignant than the question of sex before marriage".[6] Fourier's critics accused him of desiring to substitute for honourable and regular relations between the sexes absolute licence, ignominious promiscuity, and some even claimed that "le mot qu'on lisait autrefois sur un palais de Ferrare, *Orgia* devrait etre écrit sur le fronton de son phalanstère".[7]

Fourier strenuously denies that "une théorie de libre amour" is necessarily a theory of obscenity,[8] and that free love will lead to scandal and depravity.[9] Indeed, he maintains that the liberation of the sexual impulse will improve relations among the sexes and act as a cohesive link between the different classes, increase production, and so lead to industrial and general well-being.[10]

Adults over eighteen will select and enrol within one of three "Corporations Amoureuses": (1) "Les épouses", who take one spouse in perpetuity, "selon la méthode civilisée"; (2) "les Damoiselles ou demi-Dames" who may change partners, provided they only take on one at a time; and (3) "les Galantes", whose standards are even less rigorous. These divisions however are in no way permanent, for he adds: "Toute femme change à volonté de corporation."[11]

But here Fourier contradicts himself. He is anxious that there should be no divergence between the practices of adults and of children. Indeed, he frequently criticizes the educational system of his time for teaching different values to children which they would not be expected to practice in adult life.[12] Logically therefore, Fourier might be expected to have preached complete sexual licence for children. In fact, beneath the lip service which he pays to liberty, his recommendations add up to a system designed to restrain adolescent sexual freedom. His proposals are in fact much more conventional than he realized. For, as Professor Dautry has rightly pointed out, "loin de prêcher une effrénée licence sexuelle, Fourier se préoccupe ainsi de retarder chez les adolescents l'apparition des besoins sexuels".[13]

Fourier recognizes love as an important passion and motivator in human activity.[14] As with all other passions he wishes to use it to allow free development of the individual, and to cause this passion to produce harmony instead of conflict.

Fourier's ideal is that all children should remain chaste until about twenty, because he wishes them to use their energies for more fruitful and socially useful industrial activities. So at the age of fifteen or sixteen all children automatically enrol in the Corporation of Vestals, who practise chastity. This corporation enjoys numerous privileges and high esteem within the phalange. Its members lead ceremonies and take a prominent part in public works within the industrial armies.

The Vestal Virgins have since Roman times "exercised a

powerful fascination on historians and novelists alike".¹⁵ Fourier was clearly influenced by them and he utilizes Roman ideas in his own scheme. The Roman Vestal Virgins "had the heavy responsibility of ensuring that the sacred fire in the temple of Vesta never went out, and their presence was necessary at a number of the most deeply-rooted religious ceremonies of the State [where they performed] many vital religious functions, all concerned with the earth and the fundamentals of living, which they alone could perform".¹⁶ Likewise, Fourier wished to make the Vestalat in Harmony an object of popular idolatry, a class of persons intermediate between man and divinity, a semi-religious caste in whose care the morals of the country would be entrusted.¹⁷

The Vestals are lodged separately,¹⁸ but are not otherwise segregated from the rest of the community. The only difference is that they must take a leading part in all socially useful activities. They must also go to bed earlier in order to get up earlier. Therefore their friendly relations with the opposite sex take place when they get up at half past three in the morning—when they have a quarter of an hour free.¹⁹ They of course see members of the opposite sex in their industrial activities, but the relationship then is that the Vestals work harder than everybody else and so win admiration. They are the chaste Stakhanovites of Fourier's industry. In such conditions they are not likely to be seduced, but their example will spread chastity among their admirers.²⁰ A young man who particularly admires a Vestal will remain chaste in order to win her.

Fourier argues that the coming together of large numbers of people during the industrial campaigns will bring the different classes closer together and create social harmony. "L'amour", he maintains, is a formidable means of forming links between the upper and lower classes. First love is eulogized, he says, for first impressions remain imprinted on the memory for life, another reason for utilizing "l'amour . . . en politique sociale".²¹ And so he is especially keen that ordinary folk should find titled people for their first love; and that the titled, particularly those of princely rank, should find the inferior in rank extremely attractive. In this way, the passion of love will not only promote virtue and industry, but will also bring about closer social intercourse among the different classes.²²

I

The good and virtuous behaviour of the members of the Vestalat will not go unrewarded. "Le petit retard de trois ou quatre ans en exercice d'amour leur vaudra toujours des chances d'accroissement en fortunes, en vigueur, en considération."[23] Apart from the opportunities of receiving the attention and admiration of the opposite sex, who might be a magnate, prince or princess, they may attain promotion within their corps. They may also find pleasure and satisfaction in the heightened opportunities for study, for the widening of their horizon, and for increasing their physical dexterity and bodily fitness.

Though all children start as Vestals and are encouraged by these privileges to remain so, Fourier calculates that probably about a half will be unable to maintain their chastity.[24] As soon as they lose their virtue, they must join the corporation of the Damoisellat.[25] There will always be, he maintains, those who because of lack of talent, beauty, character, or temperament, will early enrol with the Damoiseaux. He believes that the weaker characters, unable to control themselves, will first succumb to temptation and desert the Vestalat. There will be others who through lack of beauty or talent, finding little scope in the Vestalat, will lose patience and escape.[26]

Fourier is emphatic that these fallen youths need not be a loss to the community. Indeed the purpose of the corporation of Damoisellat is to make these youths and maidens as respectable as possible. The phalange will clearly look upon them as fallen creatures less admirable than the Vestals, but Fourier's aim is that they should not feel ashamed of themselves, nor become outcasts of the community.

This corporation will thus strive to maintain high ideals among these fallen youths. They will be helped and encouraged to pursue happy and useful lives, and to continue to render useful service to the community. The Damoisellat will encourage decency and decorum in relations among themselves. They will be strongly encouraged to remain faithful to their partner throughout their youth. Fidelity will thus be encouraged, and reward for fidelity will be privileged admission to the army. The sanction of infidelity is relegation to a lower class without privileges—a matter which Fourier does not expound.

What therefore Fourier advocates is 'going steady', 'boy

friends' and 'girl friends'. As far as possible, he tries to channel the mixing of the sexes into communal activities with profitable purposes. In modern times, these would mean "mixed games and pursuits", in his system it is emulation in industry.

One of the reasons Fourier gives for demanding chastity of children of sixteen is that its absence leads to a fall in industrial output. It would be a bad example for the very young to see older children lying late in bed. Corruption would gradually spread until it reached children of fourteen or thirteen. It is therefore necessary to maintain the ideal of the Vestal.[27]

Fourier therefore offers no programme of sex education. Though on one hand he wishes to use love for good purposes, he nevertheless does not wish to give it free course in adolescence, as he does with the other passions. He hopes to produce "disdain" for love and divert the attention of children to other pursuits.[28]

And yet surprisingly, Fourier is against any form of sexual education before puberty. He is not aware that education in sexual matters should be a gradual and continuous process,[29] nor does he subscribe to the modern view that "sex information should be given in advance of puberty, i.e. well before the 'teens'."[30] The young under fifteen, Fourier argues, have no experience of sexual impulses.[31] Any discussion of such impulses are consequently meaningless to them, and it is futile to teach them about the system of nature in its theoretical aspects, and to explain to them "les jolis emblèmes de l'analogie passionnelle".[32] Children, however precocious, will be unable to understand the implications. The practical aspects must, as always, precede the theoretical; and so Fourier adds that works containing no mention of these items will need to be made available in Harmony.

The provision of ample opportunities for recreation, education, service and work for the community is sufficient, in Fourier's opinion, to prevent a premature interest in sex. He seems to believe that in Harmony, even with the sexual laxity in the adult, children will remain uninterested. Elsewhere he lays, as we have seen, great emphasis on the education of children on the farms, and yet in his discussion of sexual education he would have reproduction ignored. He even provides that "Toute chienne ou autre bête en rut sera soigneusement mise à l'écart."[33] This separation to be effected by the Coers and Coeresses, so that the uninitiated would have no inkling of what goes on!

For all his insight, Fourier has no real contribution to make to the theory or practice of sexual education. It is true that he does insist on the provision of wide and varied activities for adolescents as antidotes to exclusive preoccupation with sex. But he does not understand the sexuality of the child. He tends to confuse sex and copulation. He does not appreciate the broader aspects of sex, love, and paternity. Education for living with the opposite sex is much broader in scope than imparting the facts of life. It includes the whole range of social relationships between men and women.[34] Fourier's solutions for sex education are obnoxious in too many respects, and really too fantastic to be feasible.

Fourier is, however, far more moderate than A. S. Neill. At Summerhill, A. S. Neill has been faced with a similar dilemma. Neill, like Fourier, believes in absolute freedom for all children. His pupils are allowed to please themselves, and are restricted merely by rules made at the Saturday evening meeting of the whole community. And yet Neill does not allow adolescents a free sex life with a partner. "I am not brave enough", he writes, "to live out the logical argument that freedom in education should lead to freedom in sex."[35] Elsewhere Neill writes: "I know of no argument against youth's love life that holds water. Nearly every argument is based on repressed emotion or hate of life—the religious, the moral, the expedient, the arbitrary, the pornographic. None answer the question why nature gave man a strong sex instinct, if youth is to be forbidden to use it unless sanctioned by the elders of society. Those elders, some of them, have shares in companies that run films full of sex appeal, or in companies that sell all sorts of cosmetics to make girls more delectable to boys, or companies that publish magazines which make sadistic pictures and stories a magnet to their readers.

"I know that adolescent sex life is not practical to-day. But my opinion is that it is the right way to tomorrow's health. I can *write* this, but if in Summerhill I approve of my adolescent pupils sleeping together, my school would be suppressed by the authorities. I am thinking of the long tomorrow when society will have realized how dangerous sex repression is."[36]

Fourier, despite his reputation, never envisaged such liberty even as an ideal. There are those who claim that Fourier is a precursor. Certainly he is outstanding among early educationalists in considering the problem of sex as an emotion. But there is no evidence that he considered sex as the principal or basic factor in the psychological make-up of man in any way which anticipated Freud and his successors.

1. U. U., iv, 217.
2. Q. M., 215.
3. Q. M., 170. It is interesting to compare this with a modern view expressed in the recent pamphlet edited by Dr. A Heron, *Towards a Quaker View of Sex* (1963). "Unconsciously both men and women are polygamous and promiscuous, as a result of drives usually kept in check by restraint which may itself be weakened by many factors of which the person concerned is unaware." 19. This statement, of course, in no way implies that the authors believe that polygamy or promiscuity is either desirable or inevitable.
4. E. Dessignolle, *Le féminisme d'après la doctrine de Charles Fourier* (1903).
5. See A. J. Booth's strictures in the *Fortnightly Review* (1872), 691.
6. *Getting Married* (1960), 75. A B.M.A. pamphlet.
7. V. Hennequin, *Les Amours au Phalanstère* (1849), 3.
8. U. U., iv, 461.
9. U. U., iv, 267.
10. Q. M., 155.
11. Q. M., 140.
12. U. U., iv, 202; N. M., 169.
13. J. Dautry, "Fourier et Les Questions d'Education" in *Revue Internationale de Philosophie* (1962), 259. Compare E. Lebouck, "Psychologie et Morale dans l'oeuvre de Charles Fourier", in *Revue des Sciences Humaines* (1962), 423-37.
14. Q. M., 132.
15. J. P. V. D. Balsdon, *Roman Women: their history and habits* (1962), 235.
16. Ibid., 235 and 237.
17. U. U., iv, 229-30; N. M., 228. "Le vestalat a la garde du feu sacré, celui des vertus cardinales." "En Harmonie on leur confie la garde du feu sacré spirituel, elles ont pour emploi la garantie de vérité et d'honneur en relations amoureuses, et surtout en paternité."
18. U. U., iv, 223.
19. U. U., iv, 123-224.
20. U. U., iv, 252.
21. U. U., iv, 262.
22. U. U., iv, 466.
23. U. U., iv, 255.
24. U. U., iv, 250.

25. U. U., iv, 222.
26. Fourier estimates that the Vestalat will be dominated by girls in the ratio of two to one, with a majority of boys in the same ratio within the Damoisellat.
27. U. U., iv, 250.
28. U. U., iv, 251.
29. See *Some notes on Sex Education* (L.C.C., 1949), 5.
30. *Towards a Quaker View of Sex* (1963), 14.
31. Compare this with Anna Freud, who has written: "Psycho-analysis asserts that the sexual instincts of man do not suddenly awaken between the thirteenth and fifteenth year, i.e. at puberty, but operate from the outset of the child's development, change gradually from one form to another, progress from one stage to another, until at last adult sexual life is achieved as the final result of this long series of developments." Anna Freud, *Introduction to Psycho-Analysis for Teachers* (1949), 69.
32. U. U., iv, 132.
33. Manus. (1852), 190.
34. See for example, K. C. Barnes, *He and She* (1962); also K. Walker and P. Fletcher, *Sex and Society* (1962).
35. *Hearts not Heads in the School* (1944), 82.
36. *Summerhill: A radical approach to education* (1962), 208–9.

CHAPTER NINE

Intellectual Education: an Approach to Academic Studies

FOURIER's ideal system dispenses with the Grammar School or its equivalent. Intellectual education is for him a means for the elucidation, improvement and furtherance of the industrial and moral life of the phalange. He does not believe in the ideal of "education for its own sake".[1] His aim is not to produce precocious savants, and so he has no time for academic learning as an end in itself. He contemptuously speaks of the scholars of his time,[2] as useless individuals capable of little else but the lining of their own pockets. Like communist scholars who view all in terms of Marxist theory, Fourier saw all which did not fit into his own framework as useless nonsense. Theoretical study, so he believes, must therefore be based around "analogies" and "attraction", the true explanation of life, as well as a practical or "mechanistic" guide to life.

Children are taught on two separate, though necessarily interdependent levels, the ideological and the practical. Fourier's ideas are essentially concerned with the basic psychological and physiological mechanism of man as he believes it was first conceived by God. He does not seek to alter it but merely to make it function perfectly in harmony with the whole of the universe.

His system of intellectual training is aimed at the explanation and elucidation of the practical and useful. He does not appreciate nor does he value knowledge devoid of a practical utility. He rejects all handed-down material and, as does W. H. Kilpatrick,[3] allows the day-to-day needs of the child and the adult community to act as determining factors in the content of the curriculum.

In so far as there must be "book learning" it must arise from the experience of life and remain closely related to it. Moreover, there must be careful and long preparation for such study; it must arise naturally as a desire, a feeling, an inner wish for knowledge, and there must be no compulsion. When the demand for intellectual study is made then it must be met.

Fourier therefore differs on this point from Rousseau. Rousseau postpones the cultivation of intellectual development and study proper for Emile until his twelfth year. During his first twelve years, he lets nature have her way and confines his training to the sensual and physical aspects of the body. Thus although at 12 Emile would know how to run, jump, and judge distances, Rousseau would have him remain perfectly ignorant. Rousseau does not really see the first stage of the child's education as a preparation for intellectual development. "Rousseau goes beyond progressive education", writes Gréard, "to recommend an education in fragments, so to speak, which isolates the faculties in order to develop them one after another, which establishes an absolute line of demarcation between the different ages."[4] Emile having thus a purely sensual and physical existence, "is very poorly prepared for the rapid studies which are imposed on him".[5]

Fourier also differs from Rousseau in giving a positive lead to the child. He sees that the child's sensual and physical development is deliberately directed to the industrial and social activities, he encourages him to see, at his own level, the significance of what he is doing. But he does not prescribe when the child ought to attend classes for formal intellectual instruction, nor does he stipulate the subjects. He leaves the choice entirely up to the child. In a footnote to one of his posthumously published Manuscripts[6] he says (almost as an afterthought) that a child will begin to frequent the school rooms around nine years of age. Before then he would normally have learnt to read and write in the "salles subalternes". But Fourier would not have worried if a child never learnt to read or never attended lessons. Intellectual learning is firmly subordinate to the desires and wishes of the child, the primary aim is development of the individual's potentialities which need not include "book learning".

When a child does however eventually decide to attend classes, this may be at any age. He will do so, Fourier believes, because of the interest developed and directly emerging from his everyday experience in the workshops, fields, and surroundings of the phalange.

The intellectual training a child will receive in classrooms of the phalange is only very briefly and inadequately outlined in Fourier's works. His views on the "core" subjects are interspersed throughout his works, but he only really deals in any detail with geography and history. Likewise, his attempts to develop and systematize a general "method of teaching" remain confused and brief. Nevertheless, we now give an account of his views on teaching of the "core" subjects, followed by an analysis of his "teaching method".

Fourier's approach to geography, as well as to the content and method of instruction of the subject, is in keeping with his general utilitarian and essentially practical attitude. Fourier turns geographical studies into a practical course for commercial and technical students.

Fourier's interest in geography had led him to publish in 1827 a pamphlet, 15 pages long, on the teaching of geography: *Mnémonique géographique ou méthode pour apprendre en peu de leçons la géographie, la statistique et la politique*.[7] This was his one practical effort to influence teaching method in the civilized world. He had inserted a notice on the last page indicating his willingness to give private tuition. "L'inventeur de cette méthode se rendra chez des personnes qui le feront appeler, et joindra, au besoin, d'autres branches d'enseignement aux trois ici proposées." There is no evidence that he ever had replies to this advertisement.

Fourier's intention in writing *Mnémonique géographique* was to clarify and explain financial, commercial, military and foreign affairs to statesmen, investors and businessmen. He also claimed that his course of lessons would be particularly useful to the offspring of the rich families of Paris, who ought to understand the working of the stock exchange, and be capable of judging the credit standing of foreign governments, "sans recourir aux opinions contradictoires des journaux qui, selon les convenances de parti, exagèrent ou déguisent les facultés de l'Etat emprunteur".[8] He thus believes that politics, statistics and geography, or what we now call geo-politics, are as fundamental to the understanding of the events of the day as they are to any sane policy of investment.

Fourier disdains physical geography, and criticizes the Parisian method of teaching as not sufficiently practical and too long in duration. The courses which he has in mind and which he finds inadequate take, he says, a whole year and deal in detail with science, geology, cosmology, but omit two essential branches of the subject. These neglected branches, which Fourier claims are unknown to the professors, are commercial policy and external politics. In support of his thesis he gives an example which he thinks is convincing. Louis XVI, although very learned "dans la Géographie physique et routinière" had no notion of "la Géographie spéculative et naturelle", and so was unable to plan for the rectification of the internal and external boundaries of his kingdom, nor for any reforms for the improvement of the climate.

Fourier goes on to recommend in detail twelve methods for the teaching of geography. Moreover, in his exaggerated way, he says that with appropriate methods of presentation, "par Mnémonique pittoresque", lessons spread over two months would suffice to teach all that might otherwise have taken years to learn. Professor Guiral, no doubt very wisely, does not attempt a detailed criticism of these methods, he merely writes,[9] "Nous ne saurions le suivre dans cette analyse où le burlesque se mêle au profond, sans qu'on puisse définir dans quelle mesure ce burlesque est un trait involontaire, ou une habileté pédagogique."

Professor Dautry in his illuminating article[10] acknowledges that Fourier sometimes had advanced ideas in the teaching of geography. He cites Fourier's insistence that the geographer must think in terms of natural units and discard arbitrary divisions based on conquest. But otherwise, he claims that it is difficult to find in Fourier's writings information on methods of learning and teaching children in this subject.[11]

The *Mnémonique Géographique* has nothing to distinguish it from the numerous opuscules which appeared at the time. "Le Mnémonique géographique, qui n'a jamais été réédité", Professor Dautry maintains, "ne mérite certes pas qu'on le tire de l'oubilie et du sommeil dogmatique où il gît dans quelques bibliothèques publiques ou privées."[12]

Indeed it is extremely difficult to take his *Mnémonique Géographique* seriously, for it is almost incomprehensible. Nevertheless, it is possible to discern a few interesting points. His idea of equating geography with civics, economics, commercial and military science is exaggerated but novel; and it does emphasize, what had previously been neglected and remained so until comparatively recently, the human as well as the social and applied aspects of the subjects. It is only recently that the skills of geographers have been utilized in town and country planning, diplomatic, commercial and military enterprises. His point that a child's interest is more likely to be roused by focusing his attention first on his town, locality and country is certainly valid.[13] While his harsh criticisms of the futility of "rote" work involved in learning the details of the meridian, zodiac equator, of the "great and ridiculous continental"[14] divisions are most apt. They echo Rousseau's urgency "You wish to teach this child geography, and you go in search of globes, spheres, and maps. What machines! Why all these representations? Why not begin by showing him the object itself, so that he may know, at least, what you are talking about!"[15] and they find a response in modern teaching practice. Nowadays, the meanings of geographical terms are "not taught in the form of definitions, as was formerly the custom",[16] while extensive use is made of field trips, museums and even ocean-going classrooms.

Likewise Fourier uses the teaching of history as a means of improving the understanding of human nature rather than the accumulation of information about the past. Despite what people may say, Fourier asserts that history as taught in his day does not illuminate nor clarify people's judgement, and people learn little from the lessons of history.[17] His views on history are best summarized by the phrase "history is bunk".

It is extremely difficult, he maintains, to interest children in a series of insignificant monarchs. French history to the reign of Francis I, with the notable exception of Charlemagne, is so "insipide",[18] and children become bored by such as "Charles-le-Simple, Charles-le-Chauve, Charles-le-Gros, Louis-le-Hutin, Louis-le-Fainéant, etc. . . . J'ai lu l'histoire de ces pauvres sires, et, comme tous les Français, je n'en ai rien retenu, excepté Charlemagne."[19]

And yet, Fourier continues, children do retain more of what they have learnt about the Greeks and the Romans, and this because it is more meaningful and exciting for the child. A child is by nature rebellious: he loves to hear about the seditious societies of Greece and Rome, who, according to Fourier's reading of history, were perpetually in conflict with the aristocracy, always secretly scheming and plotting against the Regents. The children are even interested in the hair styles of Brutus and Gracchus.[20]

He warmly approves of what he calls the "very sensible" proposition made by d'Alembert to teach history "en marche retrograde, allant du présent au passé".[21] This method is particularly suitable for the young. Children generally prefer to think about what they know or can easily compare. Their young minds are not yet capable of assimilating vast fields of study. It is consequently necessary to give them subjects they will find interesting and contemporary events seem most suitable. He naïvely believes that they will desire to know the causes for the occurrence of the particular events and so will spontaneously delve into the past to find them.[22] Nevertheless, he firmly maintains that no one method ought to be used in isolation, and believes it preferable that several different methods or approaches be used simultaneously. This course is more likely, he argues, to be better suited to the varied abilities and interests of children.

Fourier briefly sketches these other approaches to the study of history.[23] They rely upon an understanding of the three distributive passions, for in essence his method is to classify and compare past events in accord with these passions. Monarchs, for example, are therefore compared for their prowess on the battlefield, in the formulation of laws, for their political dexterity and so on. An interesting choice for such an analysis, says Fourier, are Clovis, Hugh Capet, Louis IX and Louis XIV. These four could be compared with Charlemagne and Napoleon: each of the four former's qualities and actions might have some relation with Napoleon's or have been determined by Charlemagne's. It might also be possible to classify important personalities in a variety of groups in accord with character, pursuits, occupations, passions, ethical worth, and so on. These classifications are more likely to arouse the interest than mere chronological accounts.

Fourier has little else to say either about the syllabus or teaching method of the other subjects of the curriculum. He hardly speaks of the ancient languages except to deplore that their lumber weighs down the natural sciences, which are full of Greek and Latin and so dazzle the women who have not studied ancient languages.[24]

There is no analysis of when or how French, French literature, or other modern languages are to be taught.[25]

Mathematics he holds in supreme regard.[26] The basic operations in arithmetic he compares with the four affective and the three distributive passions.[27] Although he gives no indication when the various topics are to be developed, one may surmise this to be when the different passions are most volatile. Addition would thus be taught during early adolescence, division during puberty. When and how progressions, proportion and logarithms are to be taught remains obscure. Algebra—"L'esprit de la science"[28]—is the most rigorous and sublime branch of the sciences,[29] but again how Fourier would have it taught is difficult to discern. Nor is Fourier of any more help with geometry.[30] Astronomy, architecture and other practical subjects which he says have a predominantly mathematical content ought to attract the mathematically able and so help develop their talents. There is no indication as to the teaching methods to be adopted.

Fourier says that in general there are many methods of teaching. In his treatise, he does in fact devote a chapter to teaching method—"Gamme simple en méthodes d'enseignement".[31] But he has neither the desire nor the qualifications or experience to discuss these in great detail, and in so far as he does so it is merely in the form of a rough guide, an approximation of the lines a teacher might follow. He is aware of his shortcomings in this respect, and of the magnitude of the task. "Un seul homme n'y réussirait guère . . ." he admits, but maintains that what he has to say will be sufficient "pour mettre sur la voie ceux qui voudront l'amplifier et l'achever".[32] He believes that it is always better to use several methods in conjunction, and to choose these to suit the ability and interest of the pupil. He gives examples of some methods which he thinks might prove appropriate.

He describes two methods, which he claims were generally approved and employed—direct and indirect analysis. Direct analysis he describes as the visual method of presentation:

divers charts, tables, diagrams are used to accumulate, classify and catalogue material. Likewise, the indirect method is for the presentation of ideas, subjects, and personalities, but this is now done 'indirectly' or alphabetically. The latter method is employed in the production of dictionaries and encyclopedias. "L'Encyclopédie méthodique est une analyse inverse composée."[33]

An alternative approach, which he claims owes it inspiration to d'Alembert, is through direct and indirect synthesis. This method makes the presentation of scientific or historical facts much easier. Direct synthesis is merely the formation of knowledge starting from simple elementary facts: in science, a start is made with elementary principles or particles and this knowledge is gradually built up to an understanding of complex phenomena; similarly in history, appreciation of events would begin in the study of the remote past and lead to an understanding of the contemporary situation. "La synthèse universelle procède à contre-sens",[34] and so merely necessitates the reversal of the method of direct analysis: complex phenomena in science are now shown to arise from and depend upon elementary principles, likewise in history events are traced back to their origins. This procedure amounts to going from the known to the unknown.

Fourier prefers the 'method of synthesis', which he claims is particularly suitable for arid topics. D'Alembert, who had first proposed its use in history, had been severely criticized because, says Fourier, he had failed to change his name to D'Alembertingham or d'Alambertendorff, for had he done so, his discovery would have been acclaimed "un trait de lumière". Fourier adds, perhaps rather bitterly, "Si l'on veut faire tomber dans l'oubli une idée heureuse, il suffit de la faire présenter en France par un Français".[35] The analytical method is suitable, he writes no doubt sarcastically, for serious, strong-minded persons, such as the Germans, who are fearlessly capable of undertaking immense labour, but light-hearted and frivolous types, such as the French, need the method of synthesis.[36] One suspects some influence by the *Encyclopédie* (1751–65) on Fourier in this context, but Fourier does not develop his ideas sufficiently for it to be possible to define this influence precisely.[37]

The three distributive passions suggest to Fourier a further three alternative methods of instruction. The first of these methods is based on "cabalistic" or group tendency, and is a refinement of the analytic method examined above. The material to be presented or learned is divided into two or more contrasted groups and then placed in a further hierarchical order, in accord with predetermined rules or definitions. The sovereigns of France and England might, for example, be classified in groups according to their prowess, in order of merit, as politicians, financiers, administrators, or placed in the order of the length of their reign, their proportional expenditure in different fields, and so on.

The "butterfly" is the second of the distributive methods outlined by Fourier and is particularly suitable for persons unable to concentrate for any length of time, or incapable of confining themselves to a single subject.

"Butterfly" minds must if they are to acquire knowledge, receive at first superficial instructions in short but frequent spells spread over a period of time. Constant repetition and revision, says Fourier, are essential if understanding and skill are to grow and develop. Later this slow start ought to lead with the more able to an increase in the complexity and depth of the instruction.

The "composite" method enhances the effectiveness of the others. This last method is supposed to make memorizing easier and understanding clearer. Logarithms in so far as they shorten the work of computation may be considered "composite". Mnemonics are, says Fourier, especially helpful, particularly when as ingenious as "comme celle du vers hexamètre suivant, qui contient en autant de syllabes initiales, tous les noms des conciles oecuméniques,

> Ni, co, e: Ni, co, la: La, la, la: Lu, lu, vi: Flo, tri.
> Le premier est Nicée ou Nicomédie, le dernier est Trente, Tridentinum."[38]

Likewise the may-flies (les éphémerides) present relationships which can be very useful in memorizing but what these relationships are he does not say. Similarly, many card and paper games ought to be adapted and used. Each piece, card or square made, for example, to correspond to some event, name fo subject,[39] but he does not say how or where these might be used as teaching aids. He is content to assert that the use of this method will make work easier as well as more interesting and shorter.

The use of analogy, as hinted earlier, explains in Fourier's system the "mechanics" of life. When appropriate and as opportunity presents itself the child's knowledge is illuminated through the use of analogy. Facts, says Fourier, will become clearer not only within the field under discussion but in a wider context. He believes that the principle of analogy is one of universal application; and that consequently it is possible to understand the unknown by analogy with the known and permissible to move from one branch of knowledge to another. "L'analogie est complète dans les différents règnes; ils sont dans tous leurs détails, autant des miroirs de quelqu'effet, de nos passions: ils forment un immense musée de tableaux allégoriques."[40] Thus, divers subjects such as planetary motion, human anatomy, and the alphabet are closely linked[41], and illuminated through study by analogy: otherwise "sans cette fidélité d'analogie, comment pourrions-nous étudier la nature".[42]

The ancients, says Fourier, had a notion of "l'analogie génerale". They had grasped a correct principle, but did not know how to apply it. They were able to show instinctively a connection between the passions and living things, but their allegories were fantastic, and in default of a knowledge of the theory of emblems, their mythologies were erroneous. What the ancients lacked was a theory of interpretation, the art of methodically explaining the meaning of each hieroglyphic animal, vegetable and mineral.[43]

The science, asserts Fourier, which will explain these innumerable enigmas is universal analogy or comparative psychology. "Elle est une des branches du calcul de l'attraction que nous avons dédaigné comme le café, pendant des milliers d'années."[44] Fourier makes great claims for his scientific method.[45] It is, he says, an immense science creating vast scope for discovery with "un million d'analogies à découvrir".[46] The accumulation of these new facts, he estimates, will at least fill one thousand thick volumes for the vegetable kingdom alone.[47] Study by analogy must, moreover, include social activity[48] and not restrict itself to the material world. In this sphere it is particularly necessary to avoid what Fourier calls

INTELLECTUAL EDUCATION

"the current philosophical prejudices" in favour of equality and moderation.[49]

Fourier copiously illustrates his method of study by analogy. He discusses these analogies, their relationship to and significance for the passions at considerable length. He displays keen powers of observation. His knowledge of flowers, birds, and plants is extensive if not always very profound. But his imagination is truly formidable. He discerns in the various flowers, birds, animals and plants characteristics, emblems or activities which, he says, have significance and parallels in human behaviour.[50]

The rose is easiest to understand for it presents allegories easily interpreted. "L'incarnat de ses pétales est bien l'emblème des couleurs du bel âge; la plante affectionne les lieux frais, en symbole de la fraîcheur de jeunesse dont elle est l'image. Son parfum, qu'on appelle mal à propos doux parfum des roses, est un arôme très énivrant, comme l'amour que peut inspirer une jeune fille vraiment pudique. Rien n'est simple dans ces accessoires: calice très orné, feuille parfumé et denté avec délicatesse; tout est charmant et soigné dans ce petit arbuste, parce qu'il représente non pas la bergère grossière, simple et champêtre, comment l'on cru les moralistes, mais la jouvencelle élevée dans le luxe, habituée aux bien séances, et repoussant les dons de la nature par les secours de l'art, enfin la pudeur en mode composé et non en simple."[51] Likewise he finds the hydrangea an emblem of flirtation,[52] the carnation a being "gorgé d'amour"[53] and so on. He finds similar parallels in the animal kingdom.[54]

In our present state of knowledge a comparative psychology of animate and inanimate objects seems to be, to say the least, premature; and Fourier's analysis must be condemned (at the moment) as nonsensical in the extreme. His revelations may be amusing, but they fail to show any useful parallelism between humans, animals, vegetables or flowers. But it is interesting to note in the work of the educator Jean Joseph Jacotot (1770–1840) an independent attempt to base education upon the principle "All is in all". Jacotot developed ideas, very similar to those of Fourier, in his *Enseignement Universel*, which was published at Louvain in 1822; but both seem to have remained ignorant of each other's work. Jacotot believed that "all human

K

beings are equally capable of learning" and that "everyone can teach, and moreover, can teach that which he does not know himself".[55] Since "Tout est dans tout", Jacotot asserted that it was only necessary to "know one thing thoroughly and relate everything else to that". In other words, no bit of learning exists entirely by itself, but bears a direct relation to a large number of related fields. It is significant also that Jacotot attempted, as did Fourier, to develop a system whereby students learnt entirely by their own efforts, and though working under some supervision, they were in fact their own teachers. In practice this implied a method of individual research or private investigation. "In Jacotot's case", wrote William Boyd, "paradox, though rampant, was kept from degenerating into impractical phantasy by the need to make his ideas work in actual teaching. Fourier lacked this check, and the result is to be seen in the extravagances of his work."[56] But nevertheless, Fourier has moments of realism and applicability.

To sum up, Fourier's ideas on intellectual education are interesting and relevant in that they emphasize the emotional and social factors of learning, and are concerned with the vast majority of children. Fourier believed, as does A. S. Neill, that emotion is more important than intellect, and he seeks to base intellectual development on sound physical and emotional basis. He sees the intellect as a tool, a help in explaining and solving the "everyday" problems of living, and not as an end in itself. Intellectual development is for him merely one aspect of the education of the child, and only a comparatively minor factor in his happiness. Moreover, he does not believe that the academic studies of his times best developed the intellect of the child, or indeed helped him to make the best use of his talents. His criticisms of the intellectual education of his time were thus directed, as we have seen, at resolving the place of academic studies in the whole development of the child. He believed that ninety per cent of children have no taste for abstract theoretical discussion and exercise. The majority will thus derive no benefit from a formal education, but on the contrary leave school with a distaste of study and academic learning.

Fourier firmly believes that it is necessary for the pupil to "solliciter l'enseignement"[57] and this can only arise from a personal interest and desire to learn. The aim throughout ought

INTELLECTUAL EDUCATION

to be the enticement of the child into enthusiastic participation and use of his talents and gifts. The methods employed have been outlined above, but in general they must be numerous, contrasted and used, if possible, simultaneously. They must, however, be in sympathetic accord with the character of the pupil and freely chosen by him.[59] But above all, they ought to arise from and be related to "life", and to the physical and mental charm and pleasure of industrial activity. Intellectual studies for the majority must be subordinate to the rest of the curriculum and activities of the child, and must be based upon a realistic appraisal of their abilities. Moreover, the studies must be practical and vocational and above all freely chosen. Indeed in Fourier's scheme for schooling we find echoed the four key ideas of the Newsom Report: practical, realistic, vocational, choice.

1. Compare the similar view in present-day Communist China. See J. A. Lauwerys, "China", in E. J. King, *Communist Education* (1963), 280.
2. U. U., iii, 390.
3. *The Foundations of Method* (1925).
4. Quoted by Compayré, op. cit., 8.
5. Compayré, op. cit., 296.
6. Manus. (1852), 300.
7. Reprinted in Manus. (1852), 267–88.
8. Manus. (1852), 268.
9. P. Guiral, "Un aspect peu connu de Fourier: Fourier Géographe et Climatologue", in *Jubilaire Zimmermann* (1949), 374.
10. "Fourier et les questions d'éducation", *Revue internationale de Philosophie* (1962), No. 60. Fasc. 2, 234–60.
11. Dautry in his article suggests that this also applies to other academic subjects. Cp. also Jules Giraud who writes in F. Buisson: *Nouveau Dictionnaire de de Pédagogie*, 648: "Fourier ne dit pas grand'chose des études supérieures. Il ne conduit guère l'enfant que jusqu'au moment où par l'exercice d'une foule de métiers on a éveillé en lui le besoin d'étayer la pratique par la théorie et de s'adonner aux sciences."
12. Ibid., 255.
13. "Geographical ideas should be based wherever possible on the home environment or on practical work." H. C. Barnard, *The Principles and Practice of Geography Teaching* (1948), 99.
14. Manus. (1852), 250.
15. *Emile*, Payne's ed., 137.
16. Barnard, op. cit., 100.
17. N. M., 26.

18. U. U., iv, 286; Manus. (1852), 252.
19. Manus. (1852), 252.
20. Once again he sees the need to make the work meaningful for the child.
21. U. U., iv, 281, 286. N. M., 221.
22. Manus. (1852), 255.
23. Manus. (1852), 253–4; U. U., iv, 286, 289.
24. N. M., 461.
25. Fourier believes that there ought to be a single language but he is not quite clear how this might come about. A congress of grammarians might meet to produce such a common language (see N. M., 18, 51, 291, 240 where he drops hints on these points), but this could take up to 200 years to perfect. Meantime, it would be advisable to adopt French as the universal language, because of "la supériorité incontestable de sa littérature" (U. U., ii, 361). On the other hand it is conceivable, writes Fourier elsewhere (U. U., iii, 261), that once inter-celestial communications have been established, the planet Mercury could provide us with "la langage harmonique unitaire".
26. "Les mathématiques [sont] l'arbitre éternel de la justice dans toutes les oeuvres de Dieu." Q. M., 417.
27. Friendship—addition; Familism—subtraction; Ambition—multiplication; Love—division; Cabalist—progression; Butterfly—proportion; Composite—logarithms, U. U., iv, 233.
28. Q. M., 160.
29. U. U., i, S. 70.
30. U. U., i, S. 187.
31. U. U., iv, 279–91.
32. U. U., iv, 279.
33. U. U., iv, 280.
34. U. U., iv, 281.
35. U. U., iv, 288.
36. Manus. (1852), 251.
37. See Professor J. Lough's Introduction to the *Encyclopédie of Diderot and D'Alembert* (1954).
38. U. U., iv, 282.
39. U. U., iv, 283.
40. U. U., iii, 214.
41. U. U., i, S., 76.
42. U. U., i, S., 215.
43. He adds "Je n'ajoute pas le mot *amoral*, puisque le règne aromal n'est pas encore connu." U. U., iii, 215.
44. U. U., iii, 214.
45. See for example N. M., 466.
46. N. M., 454.
47. U. U., iii, 227; N. M., 45.
48. U. U., iii, 231.
49. Q. M., 429.
50. See for example the tables in U. U., iii, 239–40. Here abbreviated somewhat:

"*Hiéroglyphes en règne végétal*
La thubéreuse, la galante émancipée
La jonquille, l'amour maternelle
L'heliotrope, l'esprit sordide
La tulipe, la justice individuelle
Le jasmin, l'ambition enfantine
La pensée, les choeurs impubères
La violette, les Dambins laborieux
L'oreille, les enfants studieux
LA MAUVE, l'ambition civilisée.

Tableau en règne animal
LE CYGNE, la vertu inutile
Le poulet, les amants inconstants
Le faisan, les amants jaloux
Le canard, les maris "subjugnés"
Le dinde, les amoureux
L'oie, les paysans rusés
La pintade, les gens communs.
LE PAON, l'harmonie sériere."

Also, U. U., iii, 213, where he states "que la rose est emblème de la pudeur;
la Vipère, emblème de la calomnie;
Le Chien, emblème de l'amitié."

For another amusing example see U. U., ii, 164, for his "Gamme des doits naturels avec analogies" where he compares the passions with various colours and curves.

Cp. N. M. 464-5.
51. U. U., iii, 223-4.
52. U. U., iii, 237-9.
53. U. U., iii, 225.
54. N. M., 464-5.
55. See R. H. Quick, *Essays on Educational Reformers* (1929), Ch. XVIII, 414-8.
56. *History of Western Education* (1921), 385; Cp. also Diderot in his *Rêve de d'Alembert*. "Tous les êtres circulent les uns dans les autres . . . Tout animal est plus ou moins homme; tout mineral est plus ou moins plante; toute plante est plus ou moins animal." *Pages choisies des Grands Ecrivains: Diderot*, ed. G. Pelissier (1921), 22.
57. N. M., 220.
58. N. M., 221.
59. See *Half Our Future* (H.M.S.O., 1963).

CHAPTER TEN

Conclusion

FOURIER's importance is primarily as an acute critic of the traditional system of his time. He was however a constructive critic who attempted to offer an alternative to that system, but his proposals were altogether so radical and fantastic as to be unacceptable as a whole. His ideas inevitably courted total rejection as a system. However, he did emphasize, in a highly original, if exaggerated, manner, aspects of the education of children which had been previously neglected or ignored. And so we find that if his ideas are examined individually, one by one, each on its own merits, and stripped of its fancy dress, there is frequently in them material which can assist in the understanding of modern educational thought, and particularly communist practice.[1]

Fourier rejects and scornfully dismisses what he calls Rousseau's pompous illusions of the possibility of a return to primitive nature. This he maintains is neither desirable nor feasible. Man, he asserts, cannot do without material comforts: good food and comfortable housing. He wishes to bring these benefits to all classes of society, but he appreciates that work is needed if this is to be accomplished. He thus stresses the need for training for industrial productivity and the cultivation of wide tastes among the population to stimulate and subsequently consume the goods produced. His ideal was a consumer, self-indulgent community, pursuing, as we have seen, both as a means and end, the full development and utilization of *all* the talents and aptitudes of all its members, with full equality between all professions and trades.

Fourier's aims are on a lower moral level than those of Condorcet and hardly as edifying, but perhaps more attuned to the twentieth century. Fourier's ideas have some similarity with

Condorcet's noble ideals—they both, for example, advocate universal education—but Fourier belongs to a different school of thought. The Greek hedonist Epicurus held that the way to enjoyment was by moderating one's desires, whereas Fourier and the hedonists of the eighteenth century thought in terms of the fullest possible satisfaction of them all. Fourier's fundamental postulate was thus the satisfaction of the physiological and emotional desires of men.

His aims are, in part, the aims of modern education, but he was not successful in developing methods to implement these aims. Though his aims are practical his methods are paradoxically entirely impracticable.

Fourier was concerned with giving happiness to man by fulfilling his aspirations instead of controlling or depressing them. To do this, he proposed three main methods. First, the education of the entire population with a view to establishing harmony between classes. He was thus an ancestor of the comprehensive school advocates. Secondly, he wanted vocational guidance to establish harmony between the individual and his work. Thirdly, he proposed closely linking education with industrial activity to enable man to enjoy his work.

The defect in these propositions is that his methods for their implementation are inadequate—both too simple and exaggerated.[2] Fourier assumes too naïvely that there are no human aspirations which cannot be satisfied. This is perhaps explained by another of his weaknesses; he neglects spiritual and religious longings. He does not recognize original sin. His treatment of moral problems is basically to avoid them.[3] He concentrates too much on material satisfactions. He does not seem to allow for progress beyond his systems, nor does he envisage the possibility that his phalansterians will get tired of eating gastronomic salads, delicious though these may be.

He sees too much of the child as an embryo man—a child furnished too early with many of the passions and interests of man. He does not allow sufficiently for solitary pursuits, nor does he recognize the need of individual development independent of group activities.

He reaffirmed Rousseau's principle of liberty in education. He believed as did Tolstoy that the great sin of the education of his time was that it was founded on compulsion. Fourier allowed the child much liberty but relied almost exclusively upon emulation and example as a means of instruction. He denied that those unable to emulate the more experienced and talented may give up, exhibit feelings of frustration and even anti-social behaviour. So here again, although he recognized that, in the words of N. Isaacs, "nothing is ultimately achieved that is not achieved by the child himself and the final aim is the maximum of integrated singleness and wholeness of which he is capable", Fourier appreciated as well that a vast deal depends on external conditions, but he lacked the necessary knowledge and understanding to discern, as the educator must, "what it is that needs to be favoured . . . in order that he may be able to focus all his efforts on providing—or if necessary creating—these".[4]

Fourier did however try to formulate his educational methods in terms of the needs of children. He sought to develop a theory of education which would balance the development of the mind and the body. He failed because he concentrated his attention on the education of the senses and the emotions. But it is he who first attempted to develop the concept of integration in education. He first saw that education must concern itself and actively pursue the integration of varied disciplines such as the arts, gymnastics and manual labour. These varied disciplines ought, he argued, to blend themselves harmoniously and create opportunities for all-round balanced development for all children.[5]

His criticism of the system of his time thus enabled him to indicate areas which had been neglected or ignored, and so he was able to make positive suggestions for improvement of the situation. He clearly underlined the need to make all educational activities pleasant and joyous, for both pupils and teachers alike.[6] He emphasized the importance of outdoor pursuits, and particularly mentions horse-riding and military manoeuvres. He sees great educational possibilities for children in gardening, the care of animals, in horticulture and in growing flowers. He saw the need for the cultivation of the arts, music, drama, dancing, and of the crafts, the need for developing skills in metal and woodwork.

Fourier's insistence on the education of the senses and the emotions anticipated the findings of educators which followed the impact of Freud and other students of the problem. Fourier recognized that certain personal wants or needs, insistent inner urges, when denied expression and satisfaction, court positive maladjustment.[7] Fourier recognized some of the more insistent of these urges, such as the craving for interesting and even exciting activity, and the desire for social response and recognition.[8]

Kilpatrick, Neill and others maintain that emotional adjustment should take priority over other specific educational aims. Kilpatrick writes: "Without proper emotional adjustment, little else avails in life. And the problem concerns not simply individuals. Society is increasingly finding that emotional problems arising from our modern industrial civilization affect the health of society as such. It is another instance of the principle that we are all members of one another."[9]

Fourier believed that these emotional and social difficulties would not arise in a free environment—in an environment wherein the child was paradoxically free to do as he wished but also participated in socially useful productive work. Fourier is thus particularly interesting in that he endeavours to reconcile individual freedom and spontaneity with collective responsibility and social purpose. His ideas and methods thus have similarities with those of A. S. Neill and A. S. Makarenko. Fourier shares with Neill an ardent passion for the principle of complete freedom of the individual child. Like Neill, he believes that the emotions are of greater moment than the intellect and seeks their satisfaction through unrestricted opportunity for self-expression, enjoyment and work through play. But he also agrees with Makarenko for the need to inculcate a love of socially useful labour, and the integration of the individual within the group.

Fourier's proposals for the Little Hordes and Little Bands were not dissimilar from the methods later pioneered by Makarenko, first as Headmaster of the higher primary school at Kriukoff and subsequently in the Gorki and Dzerjhinski communes. Makarenko, like Fourier, made a strong point of military drill, flags, symbols, drums, parades, decorations and badges for the pupils; but, significantly, unlike Fourier, he maintained strict discipline.[10] Makarenko "organized (at Kriukoff) the work of his pupils in the school garden, which in itself was an innovation for its time. The entire school was divided into groups, each with its own distinguishing badge, a white armlet with a device worked on it in the form of a cherry, a carrot, or an apple according to the species of plant or tree the group happened to be working on at the time. The children would assemble in the school hall, the flag would be unfurled, Makarenko took command, and the column, with drums beating and banners waving would march to the scene of their labours. Before starting work Makarenko would make a short speech and then each group would proceed to its allotted task".[11]

Later at Trepke, the Gorki community farmed some land, cultivated a large garden and greenhouse and "in addition they ran the mill, which ground all the flour for the colony and the neighbouring villages; a blacksmith's and wheelwright's shop, which served their own farm implements and did similar work for outside clients; boat- and shoe-making workshops; a carpenter's shop; and the girls had their own dressmaking workshop, besides running the laundry."[12]

All this work was organized by Makarenko in a system of "detachments". These "detachments" gradually developed—slowly and pragmatically—and remained flexible in their composition and numbers. Everyone in the commune was eventually given the opportunity to assume responsibility within some "detachment".[13] Other points of similarity with Makarenko are that he also pursued collective methods of discipline maintained by children, emphasized the importance of drama[14] and paid children for their work.[15]

But for all these striking similarities, Fourier differs from Makarenko in his emphasis on individual freedom. "It was not", as James Bowen has written, "that Makarenko deliberately denied the individual, but rather that he failed to see it as the beginnings of educational endeavour. For Makarenko the individual personality was an obstruction to the attainment of the communist state, and he directed his efforts at the primary construction of the collective."[16]

Fourier contrariwise sees the individual's satisfaction as the primary raison d'être of the collective. He attempts to reconcile the rights of the individual with the collective demands of society, and adopts a solution similar in principle to that pursued at Summerhill. He allows free choice of occupation. The child, and later the adult, is allowed (as we have already seen) abundant freedom to move between groups, but while participating within the group he must accept its responsibilities. Fourier's proposals thus differ from those of Neill in his insistence on work in groups, the superior opportunities provided by his imaginary phalange, his conscious inculcation of a love of socially useful productive labour and the close attention paid to industrial labour.

Fourier is now also recognized, particularly by Soviet scholars, as one of the earliest thinkers who first emphasized the importance of linking education with productive work.[17] Fourier influenced the "great Russian revolutionaries and democrats", N. G. Chernyshevsky (1828–89), and possibly Dobrolyubov (1836–61).[18] Many of their views on education are certainly 'pure Fourier'. They had a high regard for manual labour as a fundamental means in education.[19] Dobrolyubov maintained that labour of one kind alone results in one-sided development. "Labour that takes various forms", he echoed Fourier, "is not monotonous and fosters all round development . . ." Chernyshevsky believed that "in the future society every individual would do a variety of jobs, both industrial and agricultural. Labour in different branches of production—in the fields and at the bench, on the building site and at various crafts—would offer abundant material for intellectual growth."[20]

Fourier's doctrine had a definite impact on Karl Marx and Frederick Engels.[21] They were certainly aware of Fourier's work in detail; and although they dismissed many of his fantastic notions, and deprecated his "unscientific" proposals, they held him in high regard. Marx wrote, of Fourier's ideas concerning education, ". . . they are the best of their kind and contain some masterly observation".[22] Marx's views on education are scattered in his works, but some of them do seem to directly reflect Fourier's ideas. Marx, e.g., emphasizes the need to combine productive work with instruction. He desires to "acquaint the pupil with the basic principles of all productive processes and at the same time give the child or adolescent skill in handling the simplest instruments used in every kind of production".[23] An upbringing which includes this essential, Marx believes, will "liberate them from the monotony which the modern division of labour imposes on every single individual. In this way, society, organized on communist principles, will pro-

CONCLUSION 149

vide all its members with a chance to use their own many-sided aptitudes developed to the full."[24]

Lenin attached immense importance to Marx's ideas on polytechnical education. Lenin believed that Polytechnical schooling would be the basis for building a classless society[25] and also prove to be "an extremely important means of training the builders of a new society composed of fully developed people [who in Lenin's own words, would be] 'able to do anything' ".[26]

In the early days of the Soviet Government there was talk of "the withering away of the school"; for had not Lenin written that "a school outside life, outside politics, is a lie and a hypocrisy". These ideas strongly echo Fourier's proposals, as this quotation from V. N. Shul'gin, director of the Marx-Engels Institute of Pedagogy until it was dissolved in 1931, and a leading educational theoretician of the period, illustrates: "In my opinion there will be no school in the future communist society. The child will go immediately into social work. There he will find no pedagogues, but a work director, who will be a sufficient cultured person, and one who knows how to handle children. More correctly, we will all be pedagogues. The child will go directly from social work to industrial work, and from there to the library, where he will find answers to all the questions which interest him. We are approaching closer and closer to this all the time."[27]

Krupskaya has urged that every Soviet pedagogue ought to be acquainted with the ideas of Fourier.[28] There are indeed many striking resemblances between Fourier's proposals and Soviet educational theory and practice, some of which have been illustrated in this book.[29] But Fourier's ideas are, as yet, not discussed in the standard Soviet text-books, although Robert Owen is given some consideration.[30] The reason is perhaps that in Soviet political theory Fourier is classified as 'utopian', and therefore out of date and impractical. However, Khrushchev, in his speech to the twenty-second Congress of the Communist Party of the Soviet Union, provided encouragement to Soviet scholars to investigate the ideas of the utopians—and he specifically mentioned Fourier among them.[31]

In the West, Fourier's advocacy of an extreme transformation of society has also made him unacceptable, and so has thrown his educational ideas into oblivion as well.[32] Though these are indeed closely bound up with his politics, they are not without interest even for those who find his politics entirely repugnant. The Welfare State of the present is much nearer Fourier's political ideals than anything hitherto known. Modern society combines social concern with the maintenance of individual property. Fourier's politics to-day are therefore less of an obstacle to appreciating his educational ideas.

Fourier's educational ideas, for all their shortcomings, belong to that large school of thought which stems from Rabelais,[33] Comenius, Locke, Condillac and Rousseau, and culminates in the contemporary movement of the "new" education. His ideas have some affinity with the proposals of Froebel, Pestalozzi and later Tolstoy, Satis Coleman, Homer Lane, Neill, the "romantic-mystics" (as Mr. Mallinson has called them). Like them Fourier anticipated (in some measure) Dewey, Ferrière, and Decroly's "L'école pour la vie par la vie".[34] A number of similarities between the ideas of some of these men and those of Fourier have been pointed out earlier—though the comparisons must not be pressed too hard, for the differences become more notable the more one studies them. It is worth mentioning, however, that Fourier's name has been specifically linked with two of his contemporaries, Pestalozzi and Froebel.

Fourier praises Pestalozzi's way of dealing with his pupils: his emphasis on kindness and consideration, his ability to win their affection; and regards Pestalozzi's boarding-school as one of the best in Europe.[35] He nevertheless dismisses Pestalozzi's intuitive methods rather contemptuously[36] and shows (at any rate to his own satisfaction) that "tous ces systèmes ingénieux ne nous apprennent autre chose, sinon qu'on ne savait rien avant eux, et qu'on ne sait rien de plus après eux".[37] Fourier's acquaintance with Pestalozzi's work, however, was confined to the accounts in the *Moniteur* and casual conversations in various cafés.[38] However, as he acknowledges, Pestalozzi was handicapped by the lack of material resources, whereas Fourier's system is developed in an ideal environment. His criticism of Pestalozzi, therefore, is hardly serious and is both uninformed and unjust.

Moreover, Fourier, never a practising teacher, had no experience of the complexity of teaching, and the details Pestalozzi was constantly devising to help children learn hardly interested Fourier. Fourier held that liberty and environment were sufficient to entice a child towards learning; the mechanics, indeed the difficulties, of teaching and learning, except in the most general terms, did not attract his attention. Fourier failed to appreciate fully Pestalozzi's attempts to evolve a method of teaching and learning; he relied too exclusively on interest and emulation and failed to examine more closely the fundamental processes of the mind—the Anschauung of Pestalozzi.[39]

There are, however, many more striking similarities between Froebel and Fourier: both men were much interested in cosmological problems, both held Schelling in high regard.[40] In their pedagogical ideas, they both emphasize free activity and imitation, and bring out the educational possibilities of gardening, model making, and other practical pursuits. Charles Gide has even tried to show that Fourier influenced Froebel, but this seems very unlikely and there is no evidence for it.[41] But these similarities in approach must not be pressed too far, and are due to the fact that both Fourier and Froebel were reacting to the same influences. Their respective ideas were more than likely worked out independently of each other.

Fourier's work is too esoteric, too fantastic and as a whole too difficult of implementation. A few known convinced Fourierists, for example Jean Macé (1815–1900), founder in 1866 of the Ligue de l'Enseignement, Jules Delbrück (1813–?), founder of the review *L'Education Nouvelle* (1848–54), and Mme. Pape-Carpentier (1815–78), for twenty-seven years principal of l'Ecole Normale Maternelle, later Inspector-General of infant schools and author of many works on pedagogy, all contributed significantly to educational ideas and practice in France.[42] More recently Professor Mallinson has shown the importance of Mme. Gatti de Gamond, another Fourierist, and of her daughter Isabelle Gatti de Gamond, in the development of Belgian education.[43] Although Fourier's ideas remain clearly discernible in all their works and practices, they naturally owe much as well to other better known educational thinkers. Moreover, they all discard Fourier's absurdities and fantasies.

The direct influence of Fourier remains difficult to assess.[44] Professor Zilberfarb claims that it may be much more than hitherto suspected, and that further research on an international scale is needed to define it with greater precision.[45] Even though Fourier's influence may turn out to be slight—as it probably will—many of his ideas recur in modern educational thought. He deserves to be better known as an early educationalist of the progressive school.

1. Fourier was by no means a communist. He was all for private property and profit. Labour was to receive 5/12 of social product, the rest going to capital and management. C. Gide, *Communist and Co-operative Colonies* (1930), 139; J. A. Schumpeter, *Capitalism, Socialism and Democracy* (1959), 307.
2. Indeed, even to-day, educational research has a long way to go before adequate methods, suitable for all ranges of age and ability, become available to the practising teacher.
3. *La Fausse Industrie* (1836), 605.
4. N. Isaacs, "Piaget's work and progressive education", in *Some aspects of Piaget's Work* (1955).
5. A. Leon, *Histoire de l'Education Technique* (1961), 78; another earlier writer, M. E. Rigolage, also recognized this when he wrote in the *Manuel général de l'Instruction primaire* (17 May 1902) "Fourier a, le premier, établi que l'éducation doit être intégrale et consister dans le développement harmonique de toutes les facultés. Dans son phalanstère il fait vivre et agir l'enfant d'une vie intense et d'une action multiple. Le point de vue individuel et le point de vue social également observés. L'un n'est pas sacrifié à l'autre. La vie, après l'école, sera la continuation de la vie dans l'école." Quoted by Friedberg, op. cit., 67.
6. This last point is not always emphasized even to-day. It indeed seems ludicrous that frustrated and dissatisfied teachers are expected to educate children to enjoy and find pleasure in their work.
7. See article "Sur l'utilization professionnelle des penchants et les dangers de leur simple repression par Charles Fourier" in *Bulletin de l'Institut National d'Orientation Professionnelle*, No. 2, Feb. 1934, 33, where the editor comments that these extracts from Fourier's work "montrent, alors que les théories freudiennes n'avaient pas encore vu le jour, un sens psychologique et très fin de Charles Fourier".
8. Professor Kilpatrick claims that these are "now fairly well recognized". Fourier cannot however be said to have clearly perceived another inner urge mentioned by Kilpatrick, "the desire for security against activities and fears". W. H. Kilpatrick, *Philosophy of Education* (1963), 380.
9. Ibid., 370.
10. "This was an extremely bold line to take in those days, as the prevailing school of educational thought at that time, in Russia at any rate, was strongly in favour of what was called 'free' education and opposed to any kind of discipline, especially anything smacking of militarism." W. L. Goodman, *Anton Simeonovitch Makarenko: Russian Teacher* (1949), 18.
11. Ibid., 18.
12. Ibid., 44.
13. Ibid., 45–7.

CONCLUSION 153

14. Ibid., 55–6.
15. Ibid., 63.
16. James Bowen, *Soviet Education: Anton Makarenko and the years of Experiment* (1962), 141.
17. J. Zilberfarb, "The relationship between education and productive work in the teaching of Charles Fourier" [in Russian] in *Sovietskaya Pedagogika* (1959), No. 12, 98–109; see also A. A. Lyublinskaya, "Psychological preparation of Elementary School pupils for work", in *The Soviet Review*, April 1961.
18. I. V. Dioneo-Shklovsky on Chernyshevsky in *Encyclopaedia of the Social Sciences* (1953) Vol. III, 370; for the importance and significance of the educational ideas of Chernyshevsky and Dobrolyubov see N. Hans, *The Russian Tradition in Education* (1963).
19. S. G. Shapovalenko (editor), *Polytechnical Education in the U.S.S.R.*, Unesco (1963), 24.
20. Op. cit., 25.
21. R. C. Bowles, "The Marxian Adaptation of the Ideology of Fourier' in *The South Atlantic Quarterly* (1955), Vol. 54, No. 2, 185–93.
22. K. Marx and F. Engels, *The German Ideology*, Parts I and III (1942), 156.
23. S. G. Shapovalenko, op. cit., 28.
24. Ibid., 30.
25. Ibid., 38.
26. Ibid., 222.
27. R. A. Bauer, *The New Man in Soviet Psychology* (1952), 44; see also H. B. Acton on "Dialectical Materialism", in A. V. Judges (editor), *Education and the Philosophic Mind* (1957), 176.
28. N. K. Krupskaya, *Pedagogicheskiy Sochineniya* (Pedagogical Works) (1957), Vol. 3, 717. She does not herself discuss them at length, in fact her references, in the 11 volume Pedagogical Works, are confined to a few unimportant sentences, Vol. 3, 428, 717, Vol. 4, 202, Vol. 10, 359, 361.
29. Further interesting parallels may be found in W. K. Medlin, *et al.*, *Soviet Education Programs* (1960).
30. See N. A. Konstantinov, E. N. Medynskii, M. F. Shabaeva, *Istoriya pedagogiki* [History of Pedagogy], Moscow (1959), or an earlier version by E. N. Medynskii, *Istoria Pedagogiki*, Moscow (1957).
31. *Istoriya sotsialisticheskikh uchenii* [History of Socialist teaching—collected essays], Academy of Sciences of the U.S.S.R. Historical Institute, Moscow (1962), 4. This book also contains Professor Zilberfarb's review article "Post-War foreign literature on Fourier and Fourierism" [In Russian], 438–63; cp. also E. Lozinski, "Fourier, Tolstoy, Pisarev", in *Pedagogichescheskiy listok* (1908), 403–11 and 481–8, which without giving direct evidence on the influence of Fourier, shows how he anticipated some of Tolstoy's pedagogical ideas.
32. Mention may however be made of the attempt in the 1840s by Hugh Doherty and others to establish a "College of Attractive Industry" where five hundred boys and girls between twelve and fourteen would be "educated morally, religiously, industrially and artistically"—but this college, as

L

far as is known, was never founded. P. K. P. Pankhurst, "Fourierism in Britain", in *International Review of Social History* (1956), 415. Doherty published in 1841 an *Introduction to English Grammar on Universal Principles*; see W. H. G. Armytage, *Heavens Below: Utopian Experiments in England 1560–1960* (1961). Cp. also the Brook Farm Institute of Agriculture and Education in Massachussetts, U.S.A., established in 1841. A. E. Bestor, *Backwoods Utopias, The Sectarian and Owenite phases of Communitarian Socialism in America 1663–1829* (1950), 238–40.

33. The similarity with the Rule of l'abbaye de Thélème "Fais ce que tu veux!" is particularly striking.

34. V. Mallinson, *An Introduction to the Study of Comparative Education* (1960), especially Chapter IV. Education for Living, 58–77.

35. Manus. (1851), 36. This was probably written in 1813, and so no doubt refers to the Yverdon establishment. Pestalozzi transferred from Burgdorf to Yverdon in 1805, where he remained until 1827. See R. R. Rusk, *The Doctrines of the Great Educators* (1954), 206.

36. N. M., 240.

37. Manus. (1851), 33.

38. H. Bourgin, *Fourier*, 62.

39. Fourier's criticism of the intuitive method as too restricting is perhaps misplaced. The Anschauung, or intuitive method, was intended by Pestalozzi to have a very wide meaning and to embrace all and any of the various stages of the evolution of ideas. In Pestalozzi's words "Anschauung is the immediate and direct impression produced by the world on our inner and outer senses—the impressions of the moral world on our senses and of the physical universe on our bodily senses." Quoted by S. J. Curtis and M. E. A. Boultwood, *A Short History of Educational Ideas* (1954), 329; Cp. F. Buisson, "Conférence sur l'enseignement intuitif" in *Les Conférences Pédagogiques* (1878), 325–63.

40. See J. Guillaume on Froebel, F. Buisson, *Nouveau Dictionnaire de Pédagogie*, 697; S. S. F. Fletcher and J. Welton, *Froebel's chief writings on Education* (1912), 4.

41. See C. Gide and C. Rist, *A History of Economic Doctrines* (1961), where Gide writes that Fourier "foreshadowed the development of modern education on several points. Froebel, who conceived the idea of the kindergarten (1837), was among his disciples", 263.

42. See M. Friedberg, op. cit., 70–5.

43. V. Mallinson, *Power and Politics in Belgian Education 1815–1961* (1963), 77–9. Mme Gatti de Gamond (1812–54) had, when only twenty-six years old, written a sympathetic exposition of Fourier's ideas. This work, first published in Paris, was translated into English in 1842—Gatti de Gamond, *Fourier and His System*, translated by C. T. Wood (1842).

44. The problem of his influence is outside the scope of this book.

45. J. Zilberfarb, *Les Etudes sur Fourier et le Fourierisme* in *Revue Internationale de Philosophie*, No. 60, Fasc. 2. (1960).

Bibliography

(1) BOOKS

F. Armand and R. Maublanc, *Fourier: Textes choisis* (with an introduction), 2 vols., 1937.
W. H. G. Armytage, *Heavens below: Utopian experiments in England, 1560–1960*, 1961.
J. P. V. D. Balsdon, *Roman Women: their history and habits*, 1962.
G. H. Bantock, *Freedom and Authority in Education*, 1952.
—— *Education in an Industrial Society*, 1963.
H. C. Barnard, *The French Tradition in Education*, 1922.
—— *The Principles and Practice of Geography Teaching*, 1948.
—— *A History of English Education from 1760*, 2nd edition, 1961.
K. C. Barnes, *He and She*, 1962.
R. A. Bauer, *The New Man in Soviet Psychology*, 1952.
E. T. Bazeley, *Homer Lane and the Little Commonwealth*, 1948.
C. L. Becker, *The Heavenly City of the Eighteenth Century Philosophers*, 1932.
C. A. Bennett, *History of Manual and Industrial Education up to 1870*, 1926.
G. Z. F. Bereday, et al. (editors), *The Changing Soviet School*, 1960.
F. Bernarcot, *La familistère de Guise, Association du Capital et du Travail, et son fondateur J.-B. André Godin*, 1889.
A. E. Bestor, *Backwoods Utopias. The Sectarian and Owenite phases of Communitarian Socialism in America 1663–1829*, 1950.
A. E. Bland, P. A. Brown and R. H. Tawney (editors), *English Economic History: Select Documents*, 1933.
L. Borne, *L'Instruction Populaire en Franche-Comté avant 1792*, 2 vols., 1949.
H. Bourgin, *Victor Considerant, Son Oeuvre*, 1909.
—— *Fourier: contribution à l'étude du socialisme français*, 1905.
—— *Etudes sur les Sources de Fourier*, 1905.
J. Bowen, *Soviet Education, Anton Makarenko and the Years of Experiment*, 1962.
John Bowlby, *Child Care and the Growth of Love*, 1953.
W. Boyd, *Emile for Today*, 1958.
—— *The History of Western Education*, 5th edition, 1950.
C. Brinton, *A History of Western Morals*, 1959.
British Medical Association, *Getting Married*, 1960.

J. A. C. Brown, *Freud and the Post-Freudians*, 1961.
J. S. Brubacher, *A History of the Problems of Education*, 1947.
Martin Buber, *Paths in Utopia*, 1949.
F. Buisson (editor), *Nouveau Dictionnaire de Pédagogie et d'Instruction Primaire*, 1911.
Dorothy Burlingham and Anna Freud, *Infants without Families. The Case for and against Residential Nurseries*, 1944.
R. Freeman Butts, *A Cultural History of Education*, 1947.
G. M. Carstairs, *This Island Now* (The Reith Lectures for 1962), 1963.
F. Jollivet Castelot, *Sociologie et Fourierisme*, 1908.
E. B. Castle, *Ancient Education and Today*, 1961.
Paul Césari, *Psychologie de l'Enfant*, 1963.
J. Charpenteau and R. Kaës, *La Culture Populaire en France*, 1962.
J. Chateau, *Les Grands Pédagogues*, 1961.
L. R. de La Chalotais, *Essai d'éducation nationale*, 1763.
T. Christensen, *Origin and History of Christian Socialism, 1848–1854*, 1962.
E. Claparède, *L'Education fonctionnelle*, 1931.
G. Coignot, *La Question Scolaire en 1848 et la loi Falloux*, 1948.
G. D. H. Cole, *A History of Socialism. Vol. I. The Forerunners 1789–1850*, 1953.
Gabriel Compayré, *The History of Pedagogy* (translated by W. H. Payne), 1903.
Caritat de Condorcet, *Oeuvres*, 12 vols., 1847–49.
—— *Sketch for a Historical Picture of the Progress of the Human Mind* (translated by J. Barraclough), 1955.
V. P. Considerant, *Théorie de l'éducation naturelle et attrayante*, 1844.
—— *Exposition . . . du système phalanstérien de Fourier*, 1845.
Emilia Cordero, *Carlo Fourier e il suo tentativo di educazione sociale*, 1920.
M. Cord'homme, *Un Educateur du seizième siècle, Saint Pierre Fourier*, 1932.
R. Cousinet, *La vie sociale des enfants*, 1950.
I. Cumming, *Helvetius*, 1955.
S. J. Curtis and M. E. A. Boultwood, *A Short History of Educational Ideas*, 1954.
Jean Czinski, *Notice biographique sur Charles Fourier*, 1841.
H. Darin-Drabkin, *The Other Society*, 1962.
P. C. F. Daunou, *Essai sur l'Instruction Publique*, 1793.
J. Debû-Bridel (editor), *Fourier, 1772–1837*, Selected passages, with an introduction by the editor, 1947.
Giuseppe Del Bo, *Il Socialismo Utopistico. I. Charles Fourier e la Scuola Societaria (1801–1922)*. Saggio Bibliografico, 1957.
E. Dessignolle, *Le féminisme d'après la doctrine de Charles Fourier*, 1903.

John Dewey, *Democracy and Education: an introduction to the philosophy of education*, 1950.
C. H. Dobinson, *Technical Education for Adolescents*, 1951.
—— *Schooling 1963-70*, 1963.
E. Doherty, *Introduction to "The Passions of the Human Soul"*, 1851.
S. Droz, *Histoire du Collège de Besançon*, 2 vols., 1868-70.
Emile Durkheim, *L'Evolution Pédagogique en France*, 2 vols., 1938.
—— *Socialism* (originally published in English under the title of *Socialism and Saint-Simon*), 1962.
Georges Duveau, *La pensée ouvrière sur l'éducation pendant la seconde république et le second empire*, 1948.
Ministry of Education, *Half our Future*, 1963.
—— *Not Yet Five*, 1962.
F. Engels, *Anti-Duhring*, 1959.
D. O. Evans, *Social Romanticism in France, 1830-48*, 1951.
K. M. Evans, *Sociometry and Education*, 1962.
H. J. Eysenck, *The Scientific Study of Personality*, 1952.
Lucien Febvre and C. Bouglé (editors), *Encyclopédie Française*, Vol. 15; *Education et Instruction*, 1939.
Vera Fediaevsky, *Nursery School and Parent Education in Soviet Russia*, 1936.
M. Ferraz, *Histoire de la Philosophie en France au XIXe siècle: Socialisme, Naturalisme et Positivisme*, 1882.
—— *Nos devoirs et nos droits*, 1881.
C. M. Fleming, *Studies in the Social Psychology of Adolescence*, 1951.
—— *The Social Psychology of Education*, 1945.
S. S. F. Fletcher and J. Welton, *Froebel's Chief Writings on Education*, 1912.
J. C. Flugel, *Man, Morals and Society*, 1962.
F. de la Fontainerie (editor), *French Liberalism and Education in the 18th Century*, 1932.
Paul Foulquié, *Les Ecoles Nouvelles*, 1948.
Charles Fourier. A complete bibliography will be found in G. Del Bo, cited above (for his published works), and in E. Poulat, cited below (for his manuscripts). His principal works were published as *Oeuvres Complètes*, 6 vols., 1841. For the sake of reference, a chronological list of the first editions of the main works is added.
Charles Fourier, *Théorie des quatre mouvements et des destinées générales. Prospectus et annonce de la découverte*, 1808.
—— *Traité de l'association domestique agricole*, 2 vols., 1822.
—— *Sommaire du Traité de l'Association domestique-agricole, ou attraction industrielle*, 1823.
—— *Mnémonique géographique ou méthode pour apprendre en peu de leçons la géographie, la statistique et la politique*, 1824.

—— *Le Nouveau Monde industriel et sociétaire, ou invention du procédé d'industrie attrayante et naturelle distribuée en séries passionnées*, 1829.

—— *Pièges et Charlatanisme de deux sectes Saint-Simon et Owen, qui promettent l'association et le progrès. Moyens d'organiser en deux mois le Progrès réel, la Vrai Association, ou combinaison des travaux agricoles et domestiques, donnant quadruple produit, et élevant à 25 milliards le revenu de la France, borné aujourd'hui à 6 milliards un tiers*, 1831.

—— *La Fausse Industrie morcelée, répugnante, mensongère, et l'antidote, l'industrie naturelle, combinée, attrayante, véridique, donnant quadruple produit*, 2 vols., 1835, 1836.

—— *Publication des manuscrits*, 4 vols., 1851, 1852, 1853–56, 1857–58.

—— *Hierarchie du Cocuage* (edited with an introduction by René Maublanc), 1924.

M. Friedberg, *L'influence de Charles Fourier sur le Mouvement Social Contemporain en France*, 1926.

E. Fromn, *The Sane Society*, 1959.

Anna Freud, *Introduction to Psycho-Analysis for Teachers*, 1949.

Gatti de Gamond, *Fourier and His System* (translated by C. T. Wood), 1842. First published in Paris 1838, and later also in Brussels, 1841.

D. E. M. Gardner, *The Education of Young Children*, 1956.

Charles Gide, *Communist and Co-operative Colonies*, 1930.

—— *Les Prophéties de Fourier*, 1894.

C. Gide and C. Rist, *History of Economic Doctrines*, 1961.

Maurice Gontard, *L'Enseignement Primaire en France de la Révolution à la loi Guizot (1789–1833)*, 1959.

W. L. Goodman, *Anton Simeonovitch Makarenko, Russian Teacher*, 1949.

G. G. Granger, *La Mathématique Sociale de M. de Condorcet*, 1956.

Alexander Gray, *The Socialist Tradition. Moses to Lenin*, 1947.

V. C. O. Gréard, *Education et Instruction*, 2nd edition, 1889.

Great Soviet Encyclopaedia, 1st edition, 1926–47.

—— 2nd edition, 1949–57.

F. Greene, *The Wall has Two Sides*,

J. Guillaume (editor), *Procès verbaux du Comité d'instruction publique*: Assemblée Nationale Législative, 1889; Convention Nationale, 1891.

J. A. Hadfield, *Childhood and Adolescence*, 1962.

A. H. Halsey, Jean Floud, C. Arnold Anderson (editors), *Education, Economy and Society*, 1961.

N. Hans, *Comparative Education*, 1949.

—— *The Russian Tradition in Education*, 1963.

Paul Hazard, *The European Mind, 1680–1715*, 1953.

—— *European Thought in the 18th Century*, 1954.

V. A. Hennequin, *Les Amours au Phalanstère*, 1849.

A. Heron (editor), *Towards a Quaker View of Sex,* 1963.
J. O. Hertzler, *History of Utopian Thought,* 1923.
E. R. Hilgard, *Introduction to Psychology,* 1957.
C. Hippeau, *L'Instruction Publique en France pendant la Revolution,* 2 vols., 1881–3.
Geraldine Hodgson, *Studies in French Education from Rabelais to Rousseau,* 1908.
—— *The Teacher's Rabelais,* 1904.
R. J. Havighurst and B. L. Neugarten, *Society and Education,* 1957.
Brian Holmes, *Problems in Education. A comparative approach,* 1965.
René Hubert, *Histoire de la Pédagogie,* 1949.
—— *Traité de Pédagogie générale,* 1946.
Nathan Isaacs, *Some Aspects of Piaget's Work,* 1955.
Susan Isaacs, *The Psychological Aspects of Child Development,* 1960.
—— *The Children We Teach: seven to eleven years,* 1959.
A. V. Judges (editor), *Education and the Philosophic Mind,* 1957.
—— *The Function of Teaching,* 1959.
W. H. Kilpatrick, *The Foundations of Method,* 1925.
—— *Philosophy of Education,* 1963.
E. J. King (editor), *Communist Education,* 1963.
J. Klein, *The Study of Groups,* 1956.
O. Klineberg, *Social Psychology,* 1961.
N. A. Konstantinov, E. N. Medynsky, and M. F. Shaboeva, *Istoriya Pedagogiki* (History of Pedagogy), 1959.
N. K. Krupskaya, *Pedagogicheskiy Sochineniya* (Pedagogical Works), 11 vols., 1957–63.
A. de Laborde, *Plan d'éducation,* 1815.
C. E. Labrousse, *Le mouvement ouvrier et les idées sociales en France,* 1949.
Homer Lane, *Talks to Parents and Teachers,* 1954.
Maurice Lansac, *Les Conceptions méthodologiques et sociales de Charles Fourier,* 1926.
A. Léon, *Histoire de l'Education Technique,* 1961.
J. M. Lequinio, *Discours sur l'éducation commune,* 1793.
London County Council, *London Comprehensive Schools: A survey of sixteen schools,* 1961.
—— *Some Notes on Sex Education,* 1949.
Paul Louis, *Histoire du Socialisme en France,* 1925.
J. Lough (editor), *The Encyclopédie of Diderot and D'Alembert: Selected Articles,* 1954.
H. G. Macnab, *The New views of Mr. Owen of Lanark . . . also observations of the New Lanark School, and of the Systems of Education of Mr. Owen, of the Rev. Dr. Bell, and that of the New British and Foreign System of Mutual Instruction,* 1819.
M. J. McCallister, *The Growth of Freedom in Education,* 1931.

Martin Malia, *Alexander Herzen and the Birth of Russian Socialism*, 1961.
B. Malinowski, *Sex and Repression in Savage Society*, 1927.
Vernon Mallinson, *An Introduction to the Study of Comparative Education*, 2nd edition, 1960.
—— *Power and Politics in Belgian Education 1815–1961*, 1963.
K. Mannheim and W. A. C. Stewart, *An Introduction to the Sociology of Education*, 1962.
K. Marx and F. Engels, *The German Ideology*, Parts I ana III, 1942.
G. Masso, *Education in Utopias*, 1927.
F. Matray, *Pédagogie de l'Enseignement Technique*, 1952.
R. Mauzi, *L'idée du bonheur dans la littérature et la pensée française au XVIIIe siècle*, 1960.
Angela Médici, *L'Education Nouvelle*, 1960.
W. K. Medlin, C. B. Lindquist, M. L. Schmitt, *Soviet Education Programs*, 1960.
Edna Mellor, *Education through Experience in the Infant School Years*, 1950.
R. K. Merton and R. A. Nisbet (editors), *Contemporary Social Problems*, 1961.
John Stuart Mill, *Autobiography*, 1873.
Ministry of Education (formerly Board of Education), *Infant and Nursery Schools*, 1933.
Ministry of Education, *Primary Education*, 1960.
—— *Half our Future*, 1963.
Ministère de l'Education nationale, *Encyclopédie Pratique de l'Education en France*, Paris, 1960.
P. Monroe (editor), *A Cyclopedia of Education*, 5 vols., 1911–13.
Morelly, *Code de la Nature: ou le véritable esprit de ses lois* . . . 1755.
D. Mornet, *Les origines intellectuelles de la Révolution*, 1933.
J. R. Morrell, *Sketch of the Life of Charles Fourier*, 1849.
F. L. Mueller, *Histoire de la Psychologie de l'Antiquité à nos jours*, 1960.
Lewis Mumford, *The Story of Utopias*, 1923.
G. Murphy, *Historical Introduction to Modern Psychology*, 1929.
A. S. Neill, *The Free Child*, 1953.
—— *Hearts Not Heads in the School*, 1944.
—— *Summerhill. A Radical Approach to Education*, 1962.
Harold Nicolson, *The Age of Reason*, 1960.
F. S. G. Northrop, *The Meeting of East and West*, 1946.
Percy Nunn, *Education: Its Data and First Principles*, 1949.
Guy Palmade, *Les Méthodes en Pédagogie*, 1953.
J. Palméro, *Histoire des Institutions et des doctrines pédagogiques*, 1952.
Pedagogicheskiy Slovar (Pedagogical Dictionary), 2 vols., 1960.
R. Pedley, *The Comprehensive School*, 1963.

Charles Pellarin, *Fourier, Sa Vie et Sa Théorie*, 5th edition, 1871.
A. Pinloche, *Pestalozzi and elementary education*, 1902.
—— *Fourier et le Socialisme*, 1933.
A. Polyakov (editor), *Osnovy kommunisticheskogo vospitaniya* (The Principles of Communist Education). Official joint publication of the Academy of Pedagogical Sciences and the Communist Party, Moscow, 1962.
Emile Poulat, *Les Cahiers Manuscrits de Fourier*, 1957.
R. R. Quick, *Essays on Educational Reformers*, 1929.
C. E. Raven, *Christian Socialism*, 1920.
Herbert Read, *Education for Free Men*, 1944.
J. Renault, *Les idées pédagogiques de Saint Pierre Fourier*, 1919.
J.-A. Rony, *Les Passions*, 1961.
J.-J. Rousseau, *Emile*. Translated and edited by W. H. Payne, 1906.
R. R. Rusk, *The Doctrines of the Great Educators*, 1954.
—— *History of Infant Education*, 1933.
Saint-Just (Ouvrage posthume), *Fragmens sur les Institutions Républicaines*, 1793–(?).
J. A. Schumpeter, *Capitalism, Socialism and Democracy*, 1959.
W. P. Sears, *The Roots of Vocational Education*, 1931.
Kate Silber, *Pestalozzi: The man and his work*, 1960.
E. Silberling, *Dictionnaire de sociologie phalanstèrienne*, 1911.
Leo Silberman, *Analysis of Society*, 1951.
E. R. A. Seligman (editor), *Encyclopaedia of the Social Sciences*, 15 vols., 1953.
S. G. Shapovalenko (editor), *Polytechnical Education in the U.S.S.R.*, Unesco, 1963.
M. J. Shore, *Soviet Education: its Psychology and Philosophy*, 1947.
Georges Sourine, *Le Fourierisme en Russie, Contribution a l'histoire du socialisme russe*, 1936.
W. J. H. Sprott, *Human Groups*, 1958.
J. J. Trillat, *Organization et principes de l'Enseignement en U.S.S.R. Les relations entre la science et l'industrie*, 1933.
V. P. Volgin (editor), *Isbrannyye sochineniya* (Works of Charles Fourier), translated and annotated by J. Zilberfarb, with an introduction by the editor, 4 vols., 1954.
V. P. Volgin, *et al.* (editors), *Istoriya sotsialisticheskikh uchenii* (History of Socialist Teaching—Collected Essays), Academy of Sciences of the U.S.S.R. Historical Institute, Moscow, 1962.
The Year Book of Education, University of London Institute of Education and Teachers College, Columbia University. 1955, Guidance and Counselling.
—— 1958, The Secondary School Curriculum.
—— 1963, The Education and Training of Teachers.

K. Walker and P. Fletcher, *Sex and Society*, 1962.
Graham Wallas, *Men and Ideas*, 1940.
W. Waller, *The Sociology of Teaching*, 1932.
Chad Walsh, *From Utopia to Nightmare*, 1962.
E. A. Westermarck, *The Future of Marriage in Western Civilization*, 1936.
A. N. Whitehead, *The Aims of Education and other essays*, 1951.
M. Wolff (editor), *L'Oeuvre Sociale de la Révolution française*, 1901.
George Woodcock, *Pierre-Joseph Proudhon: A biography*, 1956.
Alice Woods, *Educational Experiments in England*, 1920.
J. Zilberfarb, *Sotsial'naya filosofiya Charles Fourier . . .* (The social philosophy of Charles Fourier . . .), 1964.
F. Zweig, *The Worker in an Affluent Society*, 1961.

(2) ARTICLES

Ark. A——n [Anekstein?], "The School of Industrial Labour in the work of Charles Fourier", in *Pod znamenem marksizma*, June–July 1924, 247–83.
John Bowlby, "Children in the Kibbutz", in *The Guardian*, 3 July 1963.
A. J. Booth, "Fourier", in *The Fortnightly Review*, 1872, vol. 12, 530 and 673.
H. Bourgin, "La Pédagogie de Fourier", in *Revue Internationale de l'Enseignement*, 1908, vol. 55, 130–43.
A. E. Bestor, "Evolution of Socialist Vocabulary", in *Journal of the History of Ideas*, 1948, vol. 9.
R. C. Bowles, "The Marxian Adaptation of the Ideology of Fourier", in *The South Atlantic Quarterly*, 1955, vol. 52, no. 2, 185–93.
—— "The Reaction of Charles Fourier on the French Revolution", in *French Historical Studies*, 1960, No. 3, 348–56.
F. Buisson, "Conférence sur l'enseignement intuitif" in *Les Conférences Pedagogiques*, 1878, 325–63.
G. D. H. Cole, "The Educational Ideas of Robert Owen", in *The Hibbert Journal*, 1924, vol. 23, 127–40.
Jean Dautry, "Fourier et les questions d'éducation", in *Revue Internationale de Philosophie*, 1962, No. 60, Fasc. 2, 234–60.
—— "La notion du travail chez Saint-Simon et Fourier", in *Journal de Psychologie normale et pathologique*, 1955, 59–76.
C. H. Dobinson, "The French Centres d'Apprentissage", in *The Year Book of Education*, 1958, 181–90.
—— "Technical Training for the Unskilled", in *Technology*, April, 1959.
M. Dubreuil, "Sur l'utilisation professionnelle des penchants et les

dangers de leurs simple répression par Charles Fourier", in *Bulletin de l'Institut National d'Orientation Professionnelle*, February 1934, No. 2, 33–4.

Henri Gourdon, "Les Physiocrates et l'éducation au XVIIIe siècle", in *Revue Pédagogique*, 1901, I, 577–89.

P. Guiral, "Un aspect peu connu de Fourier: Fourier Géographe et Climatologue", in *Jubilaire Zimmermann*, 1949, 373–8.

Paul Janet, "La philosophie de Charles Fourier", in *Revue des Deux Mondes*, 1879, 619–45.

Lisl Klein, "The Meaning of Work", in *Fabian Tract 349*, 1963.

N. S. Krushchev, "On strengthening the ties of the School with Life, and Further Developing the System of Public Education", in *Soviet Booklet No. 42*, October 1958.

Joseph A. Lauwerys, "The Philosophical Approach to Comparative Education", in *International Review of Education*, 1959, 281–96.

A. A. Lyublinskaya, "Psychological preparation of Elementary School pupils for work", in *The Soviet Review*, April 1961.

E. Lozinskii, "Fourier, Tolstoy, Pisarev", in *Pedagogicheskii Listok*, 1908, No. 6, 403–11; No. 7, 481–88.

Emile Lehouck, "Psychologie et morale dans l'oeuvre de Charles Fourier", in *Revue des Sciences Humaines*, July–September 1962, 423–38.

I. D. Lloyd-Jones, "Charles Fourier: The Realistic Visionary", in *History Today*, March 1962, 198–205.

Vernon Mallinson, "The Development of the Idea of the 'Ecole Unique' in France", in *Forum*, Summer 1960, II, 3, 112–14.

M. G. Mason, "John Locke's Proposals on Work-House Schools", in *Durham Research Review*, September 1962.

R. K. P. Pankhurst, "Fourierism in Britain", in *International Review of Social History*, 1956, I, 398–432.

A. J. Peters, "The Changing Idea of Technical Education", in *British Journal of Educational Studies*, 1963, XI, 2, 142–66.

Emile Poulat, "Le séjour de Fourier en Bugey (1816–1821)", in *Le Bugey*, 1956, fasc. 43, 5–27.

E. P. [Emile Poulat?], "The bibliography of the works of Charles Fourier and his school, compiled by Giuseppe Del Bo" (a review article), in *L'Année Sociologique*, 1958, 227–28.

D. Miliani, "Utopian Socialism in Spanish America", in *Journal of the History of Ideas*, 1963, XXIV, 4, 523–538.

M. F. Yates, "The Need for Service"—"A Service Year", in *Times Educational Supplement*, 23 February 1962.

J. Zilberfarb, "Post-War Foreign literature on Fourier and Fourierism", in *Istoriya sotsialisticheskihk uchenii*, 1962.

"The Relationship between education and productive work

in the teaching of Charles Fourier", in *Sovietskaya pedagogika*, 1959, 12, 98–109.

—— "Les Etudes sur Fourier et le Fourierisme, vues par un historien", in *Revue Internationale de Philosophie*, 1962, No. 60, Fasc. 2, 261–79.

—— "Sources for a study of the ideological heritage of Charles Fourier", in *Novyy i noveyshi istoriya*, 1963, No. I, 122–30.

Index

Academic study, 40, 84, 98, 112, 127–8
activity methods, 73–4, 83, 94, 145
adolescents, 97–116
aggression in childhood, 100
agriculture, 88, 145
Alembert, J. Le Rond d', 132, 134
analogy, 'laws of', 20, 127, 136
Andreae, J. V., 67
animals, education in the care of, 88–9, 103, 107, 137, 145
Armytage, W. H. G., 154
art, 92, 113, 145
attraction, principle of, 9, 20, 73–5

Bacon, Francis, 41
Barnard, H. C., 31, 139
Bell, Dr. Andrew, 26, 54–5
Bowen, James, 147
Bowlby, John, 54
Boyd, William, 3, 138
Boy Scouts, 27, 59
Brillant-Savarin, A., 5, 15
Brickman, William, 14
Brincour, Colonel, 7
Buber, Martin, 4
Buisson, F., 2, 3, 46, 139, 154
Bulletin de Lyon, 7
Burlingham, Dorothy, 70

Campanella, 53
Carstairs, G. M., 106
charity, 102 ff.
Charlemagne, 131
Chernyshevsky, N. G., 148, 153
child labour, 101 ff.
China, 45
choeurs de l'enfance, 58
civilization, 14, 40, 56, 59, 71–2, 76, 90, 93, 99, 102, 108, 109, 111, 146, Fourier's use of, 14
clothes, 114–5

Comenius, J. A., 41, 67, 94, 150
community, service to, 99–106
Cole, G. D. H., on Fourier, 17
communal education, 36–7, 51, 53–4, 67, 70, 98
Condillac, E. B. de, 13, 14, 76, 94, 150
Compayré, Gabriel, 1, 3
Condorcet, Marquis de, 13, 15, 26, 35, 36, 37, 107, 143
Considérant, Victor, 12, 17
cooking, 8, 44, 78, 84–7

Dalton plan, 26
Danton, G. J., 46
Dautry, Jean, 14, 18, 120, 130
Delbruck, Jules, 151
delinquency, 99–100
dentists, 73
Dewey, John, 150
deviance, 93, 98
Diderot, 34
Dobinson, C. H., 42, 65, 79, 116
Dobrolyubov, N. A., 148, 153
drama, 91, 145, 147
Durkheim, Emile, 31, 41, 105

early childhood, 39, 67, 79
école unique, 37, 144
emulation, 74, 151
Enfantin, B. P., 53
Engels, F., 148
Epicurus, 144
equality, 21, 33, 37, 106, 143

family, 51, 69, 97
fathers' role in education, 52 ff.
Fediaevsky, V., 80
Fellenberg, P. E. von, 33
history, teaching of, 132
Fourier, Baron Jean Baptiste Joseph, mathematician, 7, 16, 26

165

Fourier, François Marie Charles, opinions on, 1–3; life, 5–9; childhood, 5; his family, 5–6; character, 6–7; employment, 6–7; his education, 7–8; interests, 7–8; publications, 10–11; disciples, 12; his appearance, 12; influence, 12–3; reading, 13; belief in God, 19–20; psychological theories and views, 19–30; his theories on, attraction, 20, society, 20–1, passions, 20–1, groups, 23–6; ideas on educational aims, 31–49; teaching methods, 51–65; on infancy and upbringing, 67–82; primary stage in education, 83–96; teenagers and community, 97–118; sex education, 119–26; academic preparation, 127–41; his importance and influence, 143–54
France, Anatole, 2
freedom, 37, 79
French revolution, 35–7
Freud, Anna, 70, 126
Freud, Sigmund, 125, 145
Friedberg, M., 17
Froebel, Friedrich, 1, 67, 151

Gamond, Gatti de, 151
gardening, 87, 112
geography, teaching of, 129–31
Gide, Charles, 11, 151, 154
Gray, Sir Alexander, 13, 17
Gréard, Octave, 1
groups, Fourier's theory of, 23 ff., 57 ff.
groups, 25–6, 56 ff., 99–100, 114; occupational, 58, 77, 85, 87, 90, 110–15
Guiral, P., 130
gymnastics, 91

Havighurst, R. J., 62
health education, 72
hedonism, 144
Helvetius, C. A., 31
history, teaching of, 131–2
Holbach, P. H. D. d', 31
Holmes, Brian, 3
horticulture, education in, 7, 88, 112

India, 45
industrial armies, 100, 108, 120
industrial education, 42–5, 74, 76, 144

instincts, 69, 71, 74
Isaacs, N., 145

Jacotot, J. J., 137
Johnes, M. H., 14

Kepler, J., 26, 29
Khrushchev, N., on Fourier, 149
Kilpatrick, W. H., 127, 146
Klein, Melaine, 116
Krupskaya, N. K., on Fourier, 149, 153

Labebat, Laffon de, 14
La Chalotais, L. R. de Caradeuc de, 35 46
La Fontaine, Jean de, 13
Lancaster, Joseph, 26, 54–5
Langeveld, M. J., 62
language, improvement of, 112, 140
Laplace, P. S. de, 26
Lauwerys, J. A., 45, 139
Lequinio, J. M., 36
Lenin, N., 2, 149
Lepeletier, M., 36–7, 47, 67
Locke, John, 13, 31, 42, 150

Macé, Jean, 151
Macmillan, Margaret, 94
Makarenko, A. S., 146–8
Mably, G. B. de, 14, 67
Mallinson, Vernon, 150, 151
'mania for dirt', 101
manual labour, *see* productive labour
marriage, 51, 68–9, 119
Marx, Karl, 2, 13; on Fourier; 148
materialism, 143–4
mathematics, teaching of, 133
medicine, 72
Mill, J. S., on Fourier, 11
Mirabeau, H. G. V. R., 34
Molière, 13
Moniteur, 13
monitorial system, 54–5
Montaigné, M. E. de, 56, 61
Montessori, Maria, 94
Montesquieu, C. de S., 13, 17, 19
Morelly, 14, 67
mothers' role in education, 52 ff., 68 ff.
Muiron, Jules, 12
music, 72, 78, 91, 145

needs, 145
Neill, A. S., 124, 138, 146, 150

INDEX

Newsom report, 139
Newton, Isaac, 9, 20
nurseries, 70

opera, 78, 84, 90–2, 113
orientation, phase of, 80
Owen, Robert, 11, 14, 67, 83, 149

Pape-Carpentier, Mme, 151
parades, 7, 106
parents, education by, 35, 51 ff.
Pascal, B., 111
passions, Fourier's theory of, 20–2, 97
Peace Corps, 110
Pellarin, Charles, 15
Pestalozzi, J. H., 13, 42, 51, 67, 150–1
Physiocrats, The, 34
Piaget, Jean, 57
Plato, 43, 53
politeness, 34, 93
polytechnical schooling, 147
productive labour, 41, 45, 56, 73, 76, 97, 120
pronunciation, 112
Proudhon, P. J., on Fourier, 12, 17

Rabelais, F., 41, 150
responsibility, 101, 105
Riesman, David, on Fourier, 101
Robespierre, M., 36
Rollin, C., 56, 61
Rousseau, J. J., 13, 14, 19, 22, 31, 34, 43, 51, 56, 61, 67, 94, 107, 131, 150; *Emile*, 35, 38, 42, 43, 52, 68, 131; *Political Economy*, 35; on intellectual education, 128; on liberty, 144
Russia (Soviet Union), 45, 53, 79, 80, 85, 109

Saint-Simon, C. H. de, 13, 14, 15
Schelling, F. W. J. von, 20, 151
self-government, 56–7, 89, 100

self-expression, 40, 100
senses, education of, 72; basic, 22, 72, 83
'series', 57
Shaw, George Bernard, 43
social charity, 101
social harmony, 33, 92, 121, 144
social classes, 33, 92–3, 102, 104, 112, 121, 144
social cohesion, 92, 106, 121
Société pour l'instruction élémentaire, 54
Soviet Encyclopaedia, 2
spontaneity, 37, 61, 146; *see also* self-expression
sex, 51, 97, 119, 123–4
sex, education, 119–25
Summerhill, 124, 148

teachers, 59 ff.; selection, 60; part-timers, 63
teaching methods, 51 ff., 130 ff.
Teddy-Boys, 100
temperaments, 70, 99
tests, 77–8
Tolstoy, L., 144, 150, 153

voluntary service, community, 104; overseas, 103, 110
vocation, discovery of, 67 ff.
vocational guidance, 43, 74, 76, 79, 144
Voltaire, F. M. Arouet, 13, 17, 19, 31

washing up, 78
Weiss, Robert S., on Fourier, 101
Whitehead, A. N., 43
workshops, 73–5

Yates, M. F., 103

Zilberfarb, J., 14, 17, 18, 151
Zweig, F., 25

/LB675.F62Z4>C1/